GHOSTS OF FORT COLLINS

LORI JUSZAK

PHOTOGRAPHY BY CHRIS JUSZAK

Haunted America

Published by Haunted America
A Division of The History Press
Charleston, SC 29403
www.historypress.net

First published 2012

Manufactured in the United States

ISBN 978.1.60949.519.0

Library of Congress Cataloging-in-Publication Data

Juszak, Lori.
Ghosts of Fort Collins / Lori Juszak ; photography by Chris Juszak.
p. cm.
ISBN 978-1-60949-519-0
1. Ghosts--Colorado--Fort Collins--Anecdotes. 2. Haunted places--Colorado--Fort Collins--Anecdotes. 3. Fort Collins (Colo.)--Social life and customs--Anecdotes. 4. Fort Collins (Colo.)--Biography--Anecdotes. I. Title.
BF1472.U6J88 2012
133.109788'68--dc23
2012025314

CONTENTS

Preface 5
Introduction 9

CEMETERY HAUNTINGS
Fort Collins's First Cemetery and the Legend of the Civil War–Era Ghost Dancers 13

HOTEL HAUNTINGS
The Lady of the Linden Hotel: She Appears Only to Children 16
The Northern Hotel: A Mother Returns for Her Child's Ghost 20
The Antler's Hotel and the Boarder Who Would Not Leave 22
Ghosts of the Holiday Inn Holidome 24
Bad Housekeeping Ghost in a Local Hotel 24

BARS AND BISTROS WITH GHOSTLY GUESTS
BeauJo's Pizza and the Avery Family Murder Speculation 26
Ivan the Hungarian Ghost and His Penchant for the Ladies' Room 29
Starbucks: An Odd Encounter with a Victorian-Era Woman 33
Armadillo Restaurant: A Lynching in Larimer County 34
Armadillo Garage: A Cursed Property? 38
The Virgin of Guadalupe and the Armadillo 44
Choice City Butcher and the Haunted Butcher Block 45
Starry Night: Who Is the Lady in Pink? 47

Contents

The Walrus Man and the Town's Most Prolific Spiritual Portal 49
Jilly Bean Java: Mother and Children Haunt the Old Underground Morgue 57
Happy Lucky's and the Gambler's Ghost 58
Moe's BBQ: The Blackboard Apparition and Her Flying Spatulas 61
The Town Pump: The Oldest (and Tiniest) Bar in Fort Collins 63
Café Ardour and the Ghost of Madame Marie LaFitte 64
The Wild Boar and Its Playful Spirits 66

Old Town Businesses: Some of Our Favorite Haunts
Frank Miller's Extraordinary Life (and Afterlife): Nature's Own Ghost 69
The Welch Block Fire of 1880 and a Poltergeist in the Present-Day Building 71
The Ghost of Trimble Court 74
The Old Town Art and Framery and the Bootlegger's Ghost 76
Happy Jack and His Long Stay at Old Grout 79
Vortex Alley 81
Déjà Vu and Our Local Firehouse 83

Local Ghosts Around Town and in Rural Areas
Suicide by Dual Gunshot Wounds in Library Park 86
The Frat House Haunting 88
Ghost Dancers of the 1800s 91
An Encounter with a Ghost Horse and Rider 94
The Ghost Who Took a Dip in the Swimming Pool 96
Old Fort Collins High School and Odd Paranormal Sights 98
Beloved Ghosts of the Railroad Station 99

Legends of the Area
The Hell Tree 101
What Lies Beneath Old Town: The Legendary Tunnels 103
A Speakeasy Frozen in Time 105
The Arapahoe Legend of Horsetooth Rock 106
Waiting Until the Cows Come Home 107

Conclusion 109
About the Author 111

PREFACE

Even a wooden coffin and six feet of earth can't hold back a story if it needs to be told. Some people believe that when a man dies, his spirit has a choice to rest or one last chance to finish old business. In a quiet little old frontier town in northern Colorado, just an hour north of Denver, the people of Fort Collins may have paid too high a price to try to maintain their peaceful small-town reputation. All through the small shops of what is now called the "Old Town" area, there are unexplained and disturbing events that remind the folks of Fort Collins that things were not always as they are now. From pictures flying off walls, to particular books that never stay on shelves, to spatulas flying out of pots and spectral beings passing through solid brick, the spirit world in Fort Collins is very active.

Wandering down dark passageways under the city, I began to think about what was next for the "ghost tour." We started a family business earlier in the year that first focused on guided hikes but quickly evolved into a business focused on walking tours in Fort Collins. There were several kinds of ghost tours we offered, but the "Fort Collins Ghost" tour was the first and the most popular. It attracted hundreds of locals and visitors from all over. One of the things we considered early in the development of the tour was the expectations of folks who would attend the tour. Most folks have never been on a ghost tour and probably would not know what to expect. Others might expect a dry lecture on local history and hearsay legends passed down through the generations. Others might even expect more of a Halloween haunted house experience incorporating props and employees dressed as zombies jumping out at them around each corner.

The ghost tour was neither a dry lecture nor an intellectually empty horror ride. It incorporated the best research we could find but also personal accounts of dozens of unexplained activities that have occurred throughout Fort Collins history. Along the way, we sometimes got more than we bargained for. The best Fort Collins research tends to come from old newspapers, especially from articles written in the late 1800s. The most spectacular stories tend to come from firsthand experiences as old-timers and shop owners share their personal accounts, from the odd to the horrifying. But sometimes we think the stories want to tell themselves. While many activities of ostensible poltergeists in Fort Collins have been terrifying shop owners for decades, little historical documentation exists to help explain these restless spirits. What is clear is that there are a lot of unexplained activities under the city of Fort Collins and a lot of stories lost forever…unless someone or some "thing" is hell-bent on telling the story, irrespective of their status in our world.

I was ahead of the tour helping out that night as an assistant to the tour guide. I wasn't really needed, as we tended to have good coverage between our main tour guides and their assistants. But I liked to come along occasionally to get a feel for how things were going and to provide feedback on how we could improve the tour. On that night, I was considering the possibility of incorporating a few carefully placed props to add to the drama of the tour. I headed toward an old underground utility room rumored to be a busy passageway for spirits between our world and some other place. The supposed spiritual passageway was through a manhole that provided access to a creek that ran under the city. As an assistant to the tour guide that night, my job was to get ahead of the tour, secure access to the room and ensure that there were no safety hazards.

As I got closer to the room, I remembered some of the stories I had heard. One of my brothers and my mom had stories of seeing things in the room resembling a person (which they sometimes talk about on the ghost tour). Several tour attendees had also reported uneasy feelings and other strange sensations after visiting the room. However, I personally had never had any experiences that were out of the ordinary after visiting the room dozens of times on various tours. The room didn't bother me, and I suspected most of the "feelings" folks got from the location were directly attributable to the fact that it was a dark, old and strange place. Anyone might feel a little uneasy in that room—especially in the context of attending a ghost tour where some folks might hope to have an encounter of their own.

Within a few feet of the door, I heard a quick shuffling noise in the room, so I stopped. Obviously, somebody was in the room, and I didn't want to run into them in the doorway or surprise them. Then I heard footsteps that sounded like somebody quickly walking away from the door. I figured this was either one of my brothers planning to give me a little scare or one of the workers from the ice cream shop above tending to some maintenance of the equipment in the room. Either way, I proceeded forward, announcing myself as I entered the room (not wanting to surprise anyone myself).

Strangely, the lights were off, so I thought for sure it was one of my younger brothers hiding in darkness, hoping to jump out and scare me. Not amused, I flipped on the light and quickly turned my head from side to side to scan the room. There wasn't anything large enough to hide behind, so I was a little perplexed to discover that I was alone. Then I quickly looked behind the door. There was nobody there, either. As I felt adrenaline quickly releasing in my body, a slight panic came over me, and I found myself unable to cope with the fact that somebody had obviously been there a few seconds ago but was not there now. Could I have imagined the shuffling sounds or the footsteps? I thought about stories I had heard about people seeing a large shadowy figure in and around the general vicinity of the room. However, I was convinced there had to be some "real" person hiding in that room in some clever way.

Not willing to retreat or question myself on what I had heard, I stubbornly scanned the room one more time. The only other possibility was the manhole that was filled with water from the underground creek. If someone had climbed into the manhole, it would have been hard to imagine. It could be done, but the hole was very narrow, and it would have taken some time to climb in and lower one's self into the water below—and then who knows what one would do from there. It was inconceivable to imagine any sane person submerging themselves into a pitch-black underground creek for any reason, never mind the fact that they would likely drown. Nevertheless, I inched toward the manhole with a flashlight in one hand and my other hand tightly clenched (half imagining something would lunge out at me from the hole). A strange thought occurred to me that we were under Walrus Ice Cream, a strange name for a shop hundreds of miles from any ocean. And here we were, with the only plausible explanation of a person "disappearing" being that they were retreating into the water below. Whatever this "Walrus Man" really was, he appears to live in the creek that passes under Fort Collins and is seen occasionally by folks in the dark passageways beneath the city.

If anyone had come up behind me at the moment I was peering into the hole and said "Boo!" I probably would have hit the ceiling. However, I knew that I was either alone or there was someone or something in that hole in the ground. I slowly leaned over the top of the hole and pointed my flashlight in it. All I could see was the restless and dark water about a foot and a half below the top of the hole, but there was nobody there—unless they had vanished into the dark waters below. Wholly unsatisfied, I quickly backed out of the room and could hear the tour coming down the stairway farther back. The room was their next stop. I thought about "warning" the tour, or at least telling the story at that time, but I was still absorbing what had just happened.

I didn't say a word as the tour guide told a story about the location and led a small group of people back into the room. I waited eagerly to see if anyone claimed to hear or see anything unusual. However, it was like any other night at this stop, and the tour was quickly off to the next stop down another dark underground passageway. My next job was to close up the room. I peeked my head into the room one more time. "If anyone is still in here, I'm closing the door now," I announced into the room just before I closed the door. I don't know whether I was satisfied that I didn't get a response from the supposed Walrus Man, but I closed the door and quickly caught up with the tour. I was also now further convinced that the tour did not need any artificial help in the way of props or actors. I just hope we never get a tour attendee caught between the Walrus Man and the path to his watery home.

—Chris Juszak

INTRODUCTION

The area where Fort Collins now stands was for thousands of years the domain of the American Indian. Arapahoe, Cheyenne and Sioux traversed this land, migrating here to the Cache la Poudre River Valley during hunting season. Buffalo, elk and deer were plentiful on the plains, and there was abundance for all.

The earliest known non-native visitors were a Spanish expedition traveling along the South Platte in 1720 searching for gold. This may have seemed like a small and transitory event, but it was the beginning of the end for the Native American tribes in the area we now call Larimer County.

Later, in the early 1800s, a wave of fur trappers of French descent camped on the land northeast of Fort Collins. The French fur traders and trappers were often on friendly terms with the local tribes, and many of the men married Cheyenne, Arapahoe and Sioux maidens. Later, in 1878, the American government decreed that all Native Americans must relocate to designated reservations, and the men who had married tribal women faced a dilemma. They had to either relocate to the reservations as well or stay in the area, abandoning their wives. Many followed their wives and spent the rest of their days far away from their beloved home.

In 1838, Antoine Janis, a young man of Creole beginnings, visited the area with his father. Years later, in 1844, Janis staked a claim to land in the valley near Fort Collins and LaPorte, calling it the most lovely place on earth. He didn't return until the late 1850s, when he became the first permanent white settler in the area. He brought his wife, an Oglala Sioux, with him, and they built a home and raised a family there.

Between the fine agricultural land in the local area and the fact that it was along the trail to California, where many flocked to join the gold rush, the area began to see an influx of settlers.

Camp Collins was established in the early 1860s in the area of LaPorte in response to what the American government viewed as the "growing Indian problem" as non-natives traveled through and settled in the area. No doubt, the Arapahoe and Cheyenne tribes viewed it as the "growing intruder problem."

In 1864, flooding washed most of Camp Collins downstream and pointed to the necessity of moving the camp to a more sustainable site. Scouts were sent downstream to identify land that might be suitable, and Joseph Mason, one of Fort Collins's founding fathers, was quick to meet them and point them in the direction of the present-day location of Old Town. It was near the Poudre River but on higher ground, where flooding was unlikely to be a problem.

Within a few years, Camp Collins had been renamed Fort Collins, and the military had pulled out of the area. The town was inhabited mainly by squatters who held out and waited to see if civilization would disappear from the area or if it would take hold.

It became apparent in the next decades that the town would indeed survive, and colonies dedicated to the cultivation of agriculture moved into the area. Additionally, the silver boom brought miners and all the cottage industries that served them (assayers, dry goods, bars and brothels come to mind). Fort Collins had swelled to over one thousand people by the early 1880s.

Many of the more beautiful buildings of Old Town were built during the silver boom of the late 1800s. Foundations were laid using sandstone from Stout Quarry, located underneath what is now Horsetooth Reservoir. Brick façades and ornate cornices graced many of the structures built during that time.

Today, as one walks through the Old Town streets, the roads have changed from dirt to pavement, but the buildings remain much the same as they stood over one hundred years ago. Rather than dry goods stores, millinery shops and bars, they now house gift shops, restaurants, specialty shops and bars. Some of the finer buildings were destroyed in the twentieth century, when they were considered just "old" rather than vintage, but thanks to the commitment and efforts of those who saw their historical value, many of the original buildings and blocks remain.

When our family moved to Fort Collins in 2010 and began to research the history of these lovely buildings, we began to interview the owners of the businesses now housed within. Our original intent was to launch a business based on providing historical walking tours, and Old Town was a great place to start.

In business after business throughout the Old Town triangle, we encountered the same amazing addition to historical stories. Building owners, store managers, employees and customers would give us the historical background as they knew it and then, often almost sheepishly, would end with: "And did you know this place is haunted?"

After the first few interviews, we began to see patterns. Businesses in the same blocks often had similar stories of hauntings. There were very few businesses along the way that did not claim to be haunted. In all, we recorded accounts of hauntings in at least thirty businesses!

At that point, we found there was quite a bit going on underneath Old Town; haunted basements, tunnels and spiritual portals over subterranean waterways captured our attention. We began Ghost Tours in May 2011 and started taking people on a journey through the history and hauntings of Old Town Fort Collins.

From the stories gained in researching for the tours, we have put together this book. Like the tours, we offer the stories in this book for your enjoyment and entertainment. We are not historians, but we have endeavored to provide historical context for the stories within. Much of the history comes from oral accounts and hearsay, and even when we've found written accounts of the same historical event, we find the accounts at odds with one another. Therefore, we ask those looking for pure history to consult with the local museum archives, read some of the wonderful history books written about the area and speak with some of the true historians still residing in Fort Collins. They are the experts.

As for the paranormal side of things, we've learned a lot along the way. None involved in the tours or this book is psychic. We are, in fact, skeptics, scientists and fact-finders. We truly didn't expect to encounter the "real thing" when we started the ghost tours.

However, the tours have often provided activity that just can't be explained away. Photos of apparitions, disembodied voices on EVPs and off-the-charts electromagnetic field meter readings where no power is provided are the somewhat scientific evidence of the unexplained. The anecdotal evidence is plentiful. The sheer number of people on tours who have been touched by something in one of the tunnel areas tells us that it can't all be imagination.

Some people are tapped on a shoulder, and some have their hair gently tugged up into the air. Women (especially the young ones) feel a hand firmly wrap around their ankles.

We don't always know who haunts the areas we visit, but based on the local history, we have our suspicions. This book is about both the living and dead of our town and how they coexist and interact.

Cemetery Hauntings

Fort Collins's First Cemetery and the Legend of the Civil War–Era Ghost Dancers

Visit the Museum of Art today and you'll stroll through innovative art exhibits in a beautifully preserved and restored three-story building. Situated in the middle of Old Town Fort Collins, it sits next to a lovely fountain park where children frolic through shooting streams of water during the summer. Such a bucolic scene could not possibly be the site of darkness…or could it?

What Lies Beneath

Fort Collins began as Camp Collins in the early 1860s. Named for the commander of the nearby Laramie Post, Lieutenant Colonel William O. Collins, this camp sprang up northwest of the current Old Town along the Poudre River. The military did not erect permanent construction on this site, and soldiers lived and worked in canvas tent buildings and just a handful of cabins. The young soldiers were sent to this post to protect early settlers and travelers from the Native American tribes, which included mainly Arapahoe but also some Sioux and Cheyenne. Early reports place about five hundred Native Americans in the general area and about fifty to one hundred settlers to start. Tension between the tribes and the settlers existed, but in general

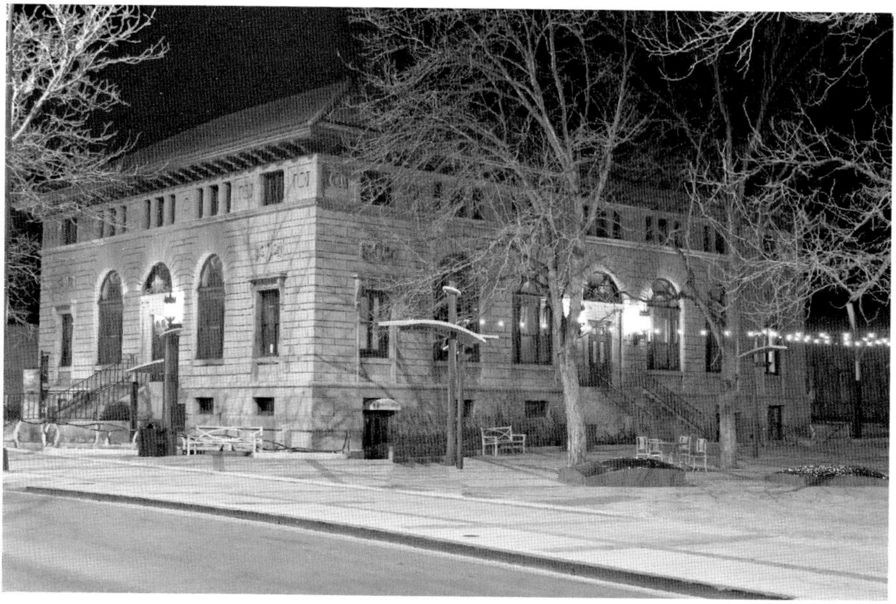

The Museum of Art (old Fort Collins Post Office).

they coexisted peacefully. While few of the Camp Collins soldiers were killed in action, a handful of them succumbed to disease during the short years in camp. A burial ground was established south of the camp to inter the bodies.

The first burial in the cemetery was one Edgarton Perry, who died in April 1863 of "black tongue." This was not an uncommon cause of death before good oral hygiene practices were introduced. In old journals, it is described as an infection of the gums or mouth that caused a form of gangrene of the tongue.

Another early burial (August 1865) was of a Lieutenant Baker, who had been sent to take bacon up to Fort Halleck in Wyoming. He was attacked by a band of Native Americans along the way, chained to the wheel of his wagon and scalped. Scalping, however, did not kill him, so the natives dragged the bacon out of the wagon, wrapped Lieutenant Baker in the bacon and lit him on fire. This finished the deed.

There is no definitive estimate of how many people were buried in this somewhat makeshift cemetery over the years. It may have been just a handful, or it may have been more. These forgotten people rested there for the next four decades undisturbed. Records were not kept, and gravestones were not installed for any of them.

In the first decade of the 1900s, the burial ground land was redesignated as the future site of the Fort Collins Post Office. The bodies were scheduled to be exhumed and moved prior to the start of construction, but alas, no one knew quite where they were or how many there might be. By the end of the process, a total of six bodies had been exhumed and moved. Only one was identified. A rolled-up note stuffed inside a little glass bottle and placed in the pocket of the soldier before he was buried indicated that the remains were those of W.W. Westfall of Company J, Thirteenth Missouri Volunteer Cavalry, who died on November 3, 1865. The rest remain anonymous to this day.

Despite the obvious concern that more bodies were likely to be buried on the site, construction of the post office began, presumably over graves. Once finished, the post office became a busy downtown hub. Stately and tall, with engraved cornices and multiple-level entrances, it was indeed the cornerstone of the community as Fort Collins grew around it.

As beautiful and welcoming as the building appeared, not all was rosy on this property. Postal workers over the years reported the feeling of being watched, and some heard voices in the rooms above when no one else was in the building. One woman on our tour said that her father was a postal clerk in the building for decades, and he felt that the building was haunted. He said that the little rooms throughout the building had a feeling of being occupied by otherworldly specters, and occasionally the sound of moving furniture would echo from the upper levels.

The building eventually became the Museum of Art. Volunteers and employees at the museum also report that the building is haunted, but they've had somewhat different experiences. They report hearing music coming from the third floor late at night and the sound of footsteps dancing to the music. When a Virginia reel is heard, they hear the shuffling sideways of several sets of feet to the beat; when the music is a waltz, they hear the gentle footfalls of three-quarter time. When someone is brave enough to investigate the source of the music, the party stops before they reach the third floor.

Some of the current employees like to think that the young soldiers and ladies who passed so early in life are up there reclaiming their youth, enjoying cotillion and dancing to their hearts' content. If you ever visit the Museum of Art, climb to the top of the second floor and pause a moment in the foyer to listen. Perhaps you will hear the party as well.

HOTEL HAUNTINGS

THE LADY OF THE LINDEN HOTEL: SHE APPEARS ONLY TO CHILDREN

Northwest Corner of Linden and Walnut Streets

A mighty Chinook wind howled down through the Front Range and nearly overturned a small covered wagon traversing the last leg of a long journey. A small group of young women huddled in the wagon shuddered in unison as they each considered their fate should the wagon be blown over along with all of their worldly possessions. Truth be told, the stuff wasn't worth much, but it was all they had left after an arduous trip across the plains.

While most settlers were headed toward the Fort Collins area to seek land, prosperity and freedom, these women were running away from lives better left behind. Women didn't have a lot of choices in the 1880s, particularly if they were of a lower station. Some took this difficult and risky trip to escape abusive husbands or families and some to put miles between themselves and judgment for some moral wrongdoing they had committed. A few of them believed that the frontier afforded them a more level playing field, where they might have more of a voice than they had in the restrictive society of the eastern cities.

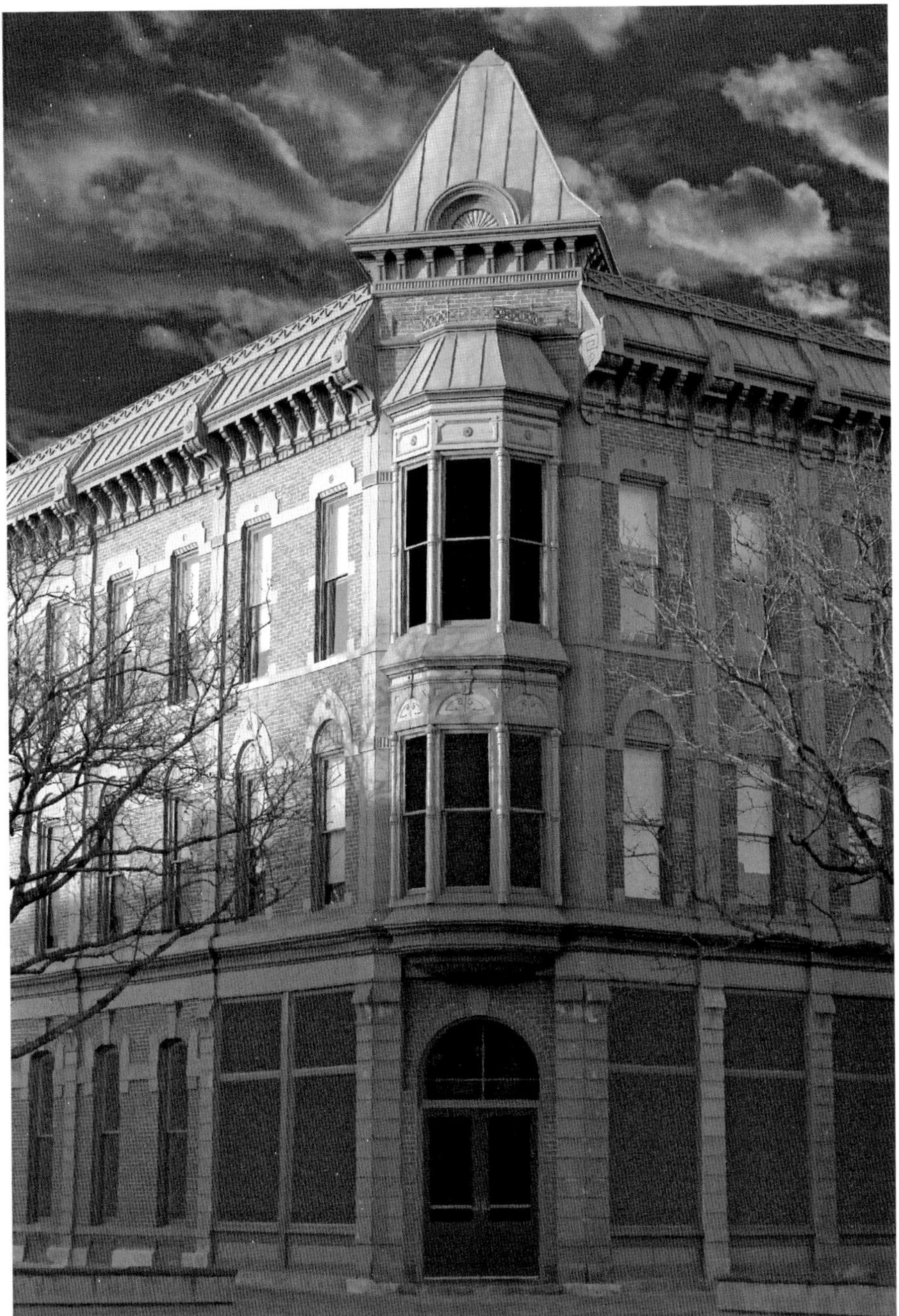

The old Linden Hotel.

As the wagon rolled into town, the curtains of homes and businesses were pulled aside as locals peered out to see who the newcomers were. If the wind weren't so wild, there would have been people out on the street, but the women arrived to a dusty and deserted downtown. Wind whipped small twisters to life in the middle of the road, and the driver of the team pulling the wagon covered her face with a scarf to avoid the sandblasting force of dirt against her skin.

Her name has been lost along the way, but her story remains as a reminder of the harsh choices frontier women were forced to make in the early days of settlement. She arrived in 1882, running from a husband with a drinking problem and a heavy hand. She had married young, wanting a family and a home. She had loved her husband, but as his drinking and abuse worsened, she realized she had to leave. This was no way to live—in fear and without love.

She loved children and more than anything wanted to be a mother. She knew that leaving him would cause a scandal and that it was unlikely she'd be granted a divorce. Her options made it clear—she'd have to leave and go far, far away to start over. Friends of friends put her in touch with a group of women headed west toward Colorado, and under the cover of a dark, moonless night, she packed a few things, slipped out of her home and climbed aboard a covered wagon bound for Fort Collins.

Soon after her arrival, she found work as a housekeeper for one of the local hotels. It was hard work, and it paid very little. She didn't quite make enough to get by, and within a few months she was thin, tired and close to being evicted from her room for nonpayment of rent. Nearly at the end of her rope, she began to look for other work.

One day, as she walked from business to business seeking employment, she noticed a well-dressed young man leaning against a fine carriage. He was whistling and watching her walk down the street. She smiled shyly, and he tipped his hat. As she approached, he stepped toward her and introduced himself. After a few minutes of conversation, he asked her to dinner. She accepted. She walked away from him feeling lighter and more hopeful than she had in years. Her life was indeed about to change.

Dinner with him was not as she expected. She had been dreaming of love and marriage, and he had a completely different agenda for the relationship. He was charming but to the point. He had money and wanted to take care of her, but there was reciprocity involved. Rather than being a housekeeper in the hotel, she would become a guest with her own room and room service. He would provide her with all she needed and desired, including a generous allowance to spend at the local millinery shop on dresses and hats. In return, she would be available to him at his whim.

Stunned at the inappropriate proposal but feeling the desperate press of poverty closing in on her, she reluctantly accepted. That night, he installed her in the hotel, and for the next little while, his gifts and attentions were enough for her. She realized she had thrown away her chances of ever being considered a potential wife, but she justified her choice as an alternative to homelessness and starvation.

Her willing affection and complete availability kept his attention through the next few months. By winter, however, he had tired of her and turned his thoughts to a new young lady. With just a day's notice, she was asked to vacate the hotel by the manager without so much as a note from the man who had kept her.

Once again homeless and without employment, she wandered about the frontier town, dragging her trunk of dresses and hats behind her on a little cart. Her new reputation as a "kept woman" prevented her from gaining honest work in a town split between bawdy revelry and Victorian morals. She asked around the local hotels about housekeeping and serving positions but was met with icy, judgmental stares. She realized she would never be offered a housemaid position. There seemed only one place willing to take her in—the local brothel.

In 1883, there were between 800 and 1,200 souls in Fort Collins, depending on which historical account one wants to believe. That year, the town supported five brothels, thirteen bars and numerous gambling establishments. She went to work in a brothel over on Pine Street, along with several of her traveling companions who had fallen to the same fate. It wasn't long before she was offered opium and laudanum, the common drugs of prostitutes during this era. Her health began to suffer and with it her beauty. Within a year or two, she was no longer desirable, and it was clear she would be turned out of her hellish career within a few months with nowhere else to go.

Her last "gentleman caller" was a cowhand staying at the Linden Hotel. She climbed the stairs to the second floor, knocked on the door and waited. He opened the door, looked her up and down and spat on the floor. "Thought they was sending me a pretty young thing, and look what shows up," he mumbled, but he opened the door and beckoned her into the room.

A few hours later, she crept quietly out of the room, carrying the cowhand's rope. She slipped somberly down the hall to the top of the staircase, where she had noticed a beam over the stairwell. She threw the rope over the beam and fashioned a slipknot to make it hold. On the other end, she tied a loop; she placed the loop around her neck and threw herself over the bannister.

Her name may not be remembered, but her spirit still remains. Oddly, she appears only to children. She stands at the top of the landing leading up from the first story in a blue dress with a pink sash, and she smiles down the stairs at children who come into the building (now a shop called Nature's Own). They are never afraid but often tug on the sleeve of a parent and ask why the lady is wearing a long dress and why she won't speak. Parents never see her, but so many children have described her in the same way that there is no question about her appearance.

Employees of Nature's Own report hearing movement in that room below the landing after closing; wind chimes tinkle, items on shelves sound as if they're being moved and occasionally something will fall right off a shelf. They also report that a beautiful glass vase sitting on one of the shelves recently split right down the middle horizontally and then split down the middle vertically and fell into pieces, right in front of stunned employees and customers.

We don't know her real name, but we call her the Lady of the Linden.

The Northern Hotel: A Mother Returns for Her Child's Ghost

172 North College Avenue

The Northern Hotel has existed in many incarnations, beginning in 1873 when it was then called the Agricultural Hotel. Travelers involved in agriculture, silver mining and settling the great West stopped to rest along the way and enjoy a respite from their journeys.

Later in the 1800s, an ornate brick building was erected, and the hotel was called the Commercial Hotel.

In 1905, however, the structure was purchased by a group of businessmen who proceeded to renovate and improve the place until it was considered one of the finest establishments in northern Colorado. The Northern boasted electricity throughout, running water to sinks in every room and beautiful Victorian décor. The dining room ceiling included a large stained-glass dome and was the scene of some of the more elaborate dinner soirées of the era.

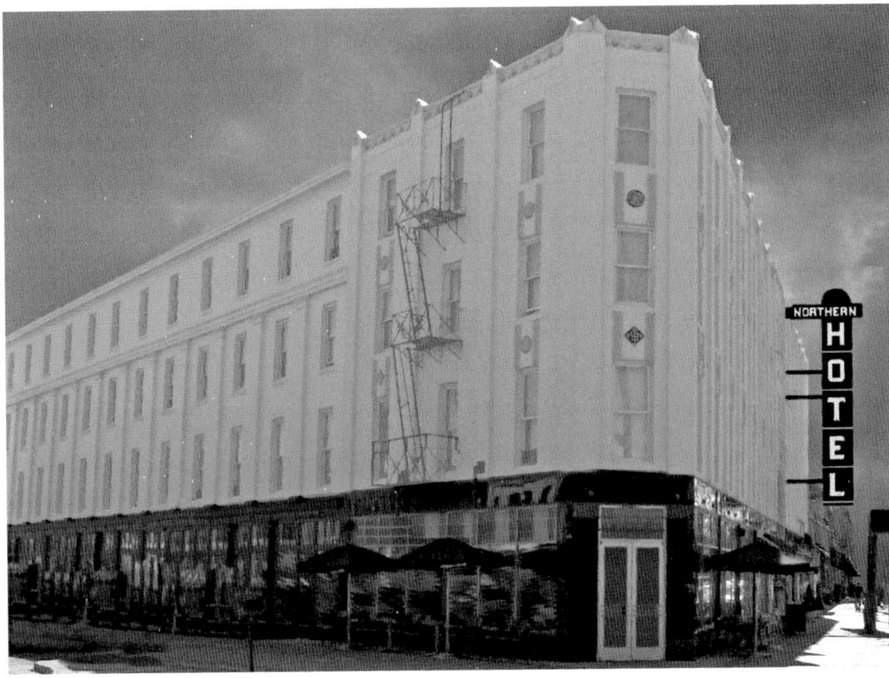

The old Northern Hotel.

A cadre of celebrities frequented the Northern over the years, and we're told John Wayne, Hedy Lamarr, Olivia de Havilland and Franklin Delano Roosevelt were among them.

There were no hauntings reported, as far as we know, during the heyday of the hotel. Then, in 1918, the Spanish flu pandemic swept through Fort Collins and cut a swath of death and grief through the community. A woman and her five-year-old daughter were staying at the hotel, and the little girl caught the flu. She fought the fever for two days but ultimately died in the hotel. Her mother was grief-stricken, and after arrangements were made, she moved on.

During the Roaring Twenties, a fourth floor was added to the hotel. The 1930s brought a restoration of the façade of the hotel to reflect an art deco theme.

Still, there were no reported hauntings for another two decades. In the middle of the twentieth century, however, visitors to the building began to report seeing the apparition of a woman dressed in clothing reminiscent of the 1910s walking up and down the hallways and peering into each room as she passed, as if she were looking for someone. Was it the mother, finally herself succumbed to death, returning to find the daughter she'd lost decades ago?

Over time, her image has faded, and her visits are less frequent. The Northern is now used for senior housing on the three upper floors, and there is retail space below. We often begin our tours in the lobby area of the old Northern, and some of the seniors have stopped by to tell us that they have been awakened in the night by a ghostly tap on the shoulder. Some have been shaken awake in the morning only to find no one else in the room. One resident of the second floor reports that he takes a nap every afternoon, and after exactly one hour, someone or something pokes him in the side to wake up. If he doesn't get up immediately, someone starts jumping up and down on his bed until he finally agrees to get moving again. He said he feels it's a female presence, and from the playfulness of the spirit, we wonder if it's the little girl.

We all wonder if the woman is still searching for her child and hope that they find each other soon in the afterlife.

The Antler's Hotel and the Boarder Who Would Not Leave

Block of 224 Linden Street

The Antler's Hotel sits along one of the original blocks built in Fort Collins. It has been the site of many businesses and often doubled as a rooming house or a one-person-occupancy apartment building.

In the early days of Fort Collins, we are told that one of the first newspapers, the *Fort Collins Courier*, occupied the first floor of that building. The upstairs floors were broken into apartments and occupied by single people and families just starting out.

A young family occupied one of the apartments on the third floor. The father worked, and the mother stayed home and cared for their small daughter. The father doted on his little girl and looked forward every day to coming home, having dinner and then rocking his little angel to sleep in their favorite rocking chair. Sometimes he would read her a book, and other times he would tell her stories, but they always snuggled up in the rocking chair before saying goodnight.

One fateful afternoon in late summer, the father was still at work and the mother was in the kitchen preparing dinner. She was distracted by the lighted stove and wasn't paying attention as the little girl wandered toward the window to look at the horses passing by downstairs. The little girl, just a toddler, leaned out of the third-story window, teetered and fell to her death.

Upon arriving home and finding his beloved little girl dead, the father turned on the mother and blamed her for not watching his little angel well enough to keep her safe. He banished the mother from the home and told her he never wanted to see her again. In fear of her husband, who seemed half crazed with grief, the mother left the home and never returned.

Neighbors tried to console the father, bringing him food and imploring him to eat, go to work or even leave the apartment. He just sat rocking in the chair, staring into space and wasting away. His grief was overwhelming, and he knew he'd never get over it.

When it came time to bury his daughter, the father dressed all in black and attended the burial at the local cemetery. When he returned home, he shut the door, sat in the rocker and slowly but surely went a little bit mad. He never left the apartment again, never changed out of his mourning clothes and rarely even ate. It took months, but his broken heart finally gave way, and one cold winter morning a neighbor found him dead, still in the rocking chair.

We take our tours right by the Antler's every weekend, but we never knew about the ghost until people on the tour told us their stories. In fact, on three different occasions, we've had people on our tours who lived in that building during the 1970s, 1980s and 1990s and told remarkably similar stories of what seems to be the same apparition.

Inevitably, the story begins with the resident seeing a man in black walking the hallway of the apartment building. He is dressed in clothes reminiscent of the late 1800s.

From time to time, this apparition would enter one of the apartments, purportedly through a closed door, and sit in a rocking chair. The resident of the apartment not only saw the apparition in the rocking chair but also the chair itself would rock back and forth for a few minutes before the apparition faded away.

Three residents from three different decades shared the same story, even though they had never met. It seems likely that the man returned to find his child. He hasn't been seen in the last few years, and we hope that means he found her.

Ghosts of the Holiday Inn Holidome

3836 East Mulberry Street

If you're visiting Fort Collins and want a room to yourself, you might want to refrain from booking a room at the old Holiday Inn Holidome, now the Plaza Hotel, over on Mulberry next to I-25. According to previous guests and employees, there are several ghosts who haunt this fairly modern hotel.

Adventurous souls, however, might find this hotel an intriguing and worthwhile stop.

On the top floor of the northwest wing of the hotel, the apparition of a man has been seen walking the halls and occasionally looking in on guests who leave their doors open.

In other parts of the hotel, a little girl's spirit manifests in front of the air conditioners, enjoying the cold air. She is playful and has been known to hide keys and other personal items from guests.

A third ghost, a woman, spends time at the swimming pool, keeping watch over the swimmers. Her filmy form and wet footprints have startled guests from time to time as they make their way from the pool to the interior hallway.

Other guests have reported hearing music in the hallways and venturing out to implore whoever had their radio on to turn it down. The music seems to emanate from the hallway itself, but no radio is in sight, and there are no speakers that could carry music from anywhere else.

Bad Housekeeping Ghost in a Local Hotel

The old Helmshire Inn stood at 1204 South College Avenue for many years. Now it is the site of Café Vino and upscale offices.

Workers at the Helmshire Inn told stories of ghosts that would follow them on their housekeeping rounds around the third floor, undoing all the good work they had done. Beds that had just been made ended up rumpled and unmade. Toilets flushed when no one was in the bathroom. Curtains that had been closed were opened right back up.

They also reported that they felt a presence in the basement, and if given a choice, they avoided that part of the hotel. Like so many places in Fort Collins, trips to the basement resulted in the feeling of being watched by some otherworldly entity.

The new building that rests on that site is beautiful and modern, but still there is a feeling that there might be more there than meets the eye.

Bars and Bistros with Ghostly Guests

BeauJo's Pizza and the Avery Family Murder Speculation

Southeast Corner of Mountain and College Avenues

On the corner of Mountain and College Avenues there stands one of the most beautiful buildings in Fort Collins. Known as the Avery Building, it was built in 1897 and first housed the First National Bank. Over the last century, this building has been a landmark of the development of the downtown area and a cornerstone of the community. It now houses office suites and, on the ground floor, one of our favorite local restaurants, BeauJo's Pizza. The building, full of Victorian charm and Romanesque arches, was conceived by Franklin Avery and designed by architect Montezuma Fuller.

Franklin Avery was one of the founding fathers of Fort Collins. Franklin came to Fort Collins from the Finger Lakes region of New York as a young man with a vision. In 1873, he conducted a survey of the town and was responsible for planning the wide streets to facilitate the turning around of horse and carriages. He changed the orientation of the streets to north–south and east–west from the parallel, matching to the Poudre River, and

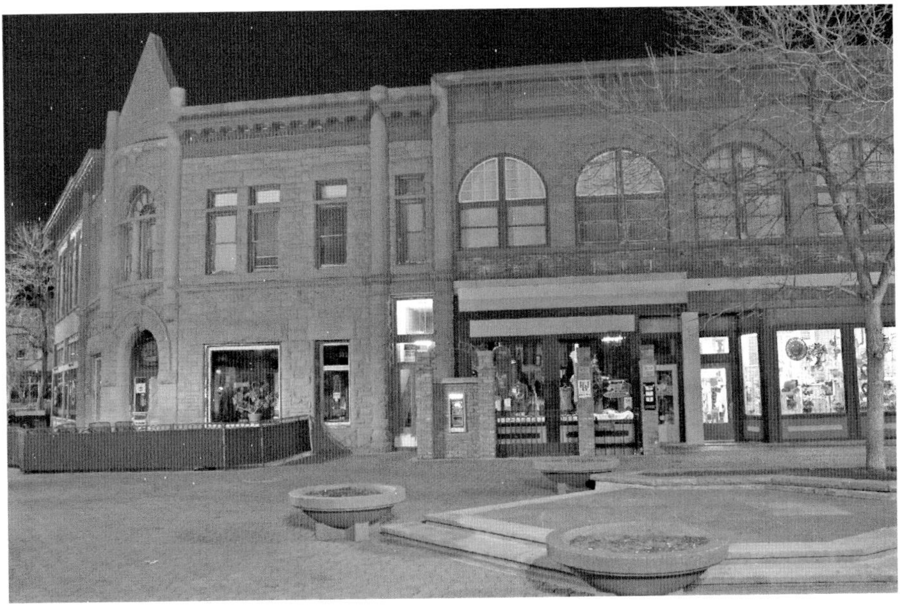

BeauJo's Pizza (old "Avery's bank"/First National Bank).

this is why Old Town's streets have a somewhat triangular relationship to the streets around them. Avery also suggested that the north–south streets should be named after the founding families of the town and the east–west streets should be named after trees.

In 1881, Franklin's brother, William Avery; his wife, Mary; and their daughter, Pearl, moved to Fort Collins as well. William was a successful and wealthy businessman. Mary quickly engaged herself into Fort Collins high society and was also the church organist. William's fortune continued to grow, and by 1890, he was worth over $100,000.

Despite outward appearances, all was not well within the William Avery family. In the late 1880s, rumors began to spread of an intimate relationship between Mary and William's business partner, Frank Millington. Frank Millington had joined William in his business pursuits in 1884, and over the years, he and Mary had grown closer. By 1890, the townspeople suspected there was more than friendship between the two, and as it turned out, they were right.

In June 1890, William was stricken with a stomach disorder that quickly led to his demise. The death was listed as "natural causes," and William was laid to rest. The community and his family mourned his passing, but it wasn't long before their grief turned to suspicion, shock and then anger.

Twelve days after William's death, Mary and Frank Millington were secretly married in Nebraska. When the Avery family caught wind of the marriage, they immediately realized that their dear William might not have died of natural causes at all. Was it possible that he had been murdered to facilitate the union of Mary and Frank?

The wealthy and powerful Averys had extensive financial and social resources at their disposal. They ordered William's body exhumed and demanded an autopsy. The autopsy revealed that, according to one expert, William had enough arsenic in his system to have killed fifty people.

Mary and Frank were arrested and, according to one newspaper account, narrowly escaped lynching by a waiting crowd. They were brought back to Fort Collins to stand trial.

The trial took place in 1891 and was quite a sensation in this otherwise sedate frontier town. Ultimately, both Mary and Frank were acquitted, as it could not be proven that William had not voluntarily ingested the fatal doses of arsenic.

The building that housed the business dealings and finances of the Averys is now BeauJo's Pizza. The building still looks the same as it did over one hundred years ago when it was the First National Bank, and the original safe still resides in the same place inside the restaurant. The basement of the building still holds the original vault where silver miners, businessmen and saloon owners stored their money.

But are the Averys still there? Many customers and employees have reported experiences in the building. There are three separate basement areas, and one is used as the employees' lounge and the office area. The door to that basement has often been seen closing all by itself, although there is no wind or any other physical force that would cause it to close.

Up in the second story, above that particular basement, customers report that their silverware will move about the table on their own, as if some otherworldly force were pushing spoons and forks from one end of the table to the other.

The first-floor room on the north end of the restaurant is on the other side of the basement from the door that closes inexplicably. Customers have seen a filmy apparition in the back corner of that room.

Often, paranormal experiences occur where unresolved circumstances remain. Could William be trying to plead his case of murder from beyond the grave? Is he trying to get our attention to let us know he was indeed the victim of foul play? Or could it be the wayward Mary and Frank, still trying to exact mischief at the expense of the Averys? We may never know.

Ivan the Hungarian Ghost and His Penchant for the Ladies' Room

The Vault (now the Astoria), 146 North College Avenue

Author's note: The Vault is the only site on the Fort Collins Ghost Tour that we stopped visiting due to paranormal activities. We work in this field and expect activity, but this place frankly didn't seem to want us there! After a break of a few months, we are once again taking tours in to visit, and so far the spirits have seemed a little less aggressive.

The Vault Bar is housed in one of the older buildings in Fort Collins. Built early in Fort Collins history, it was originally the Commercial Trust and Savings Bank. The two room-sized vaults built for holding money are still intact within the bar. One is a back room where a new art gallery within a new restaurant is being set up, and the old basement vault serves as the office for the bar owner. They are both impressive and creepy, with high curved ceilings and near-impenetrable walls.

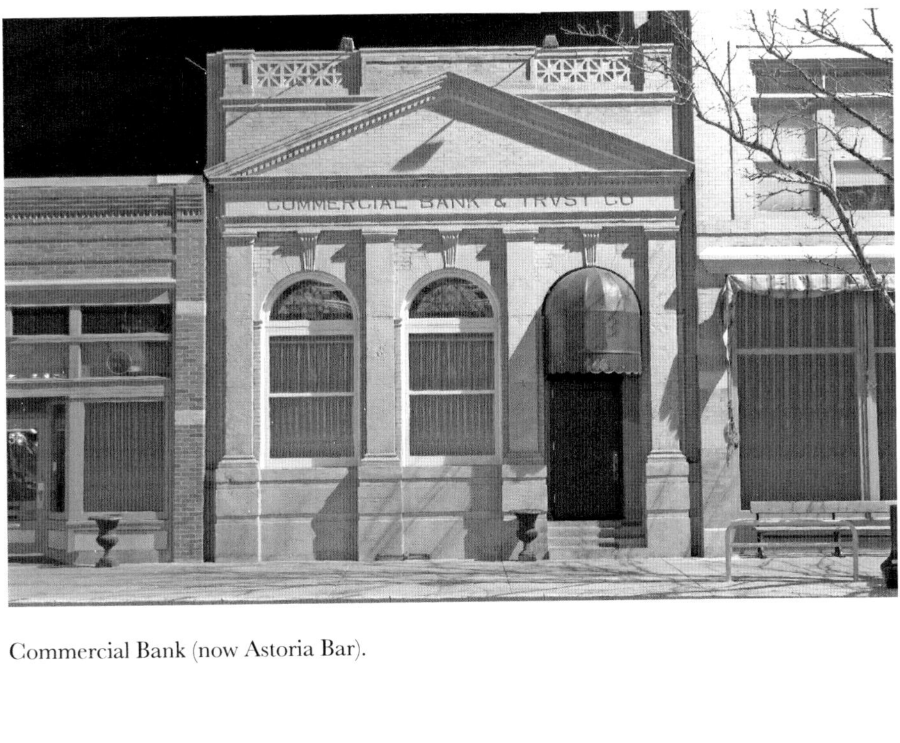

Commercial Bank (now Astoria Bar).

The façade of the building remains the same as it stood over one hundred years ago, but then it faced a dirt road traversed by horses and carriages, cowboys and silver miners, gamblers and madams. Fort Collins was a rough and rowdy Old West town in those days. The bank was one place where the business owners of the seedy underbelly of the town would deposit their "dirty money" alongside the upstanding citizens queuing up to deposit cleaner funds from agricultural endeavors and silver mining.

When Fort Collins Tours started, an employee of the Vault (LC) took us on a tour of the building and even beyond the basement, which tunneled through underneath the sidewalk and out below the main street (College Avenue).

LC told us that the owner of the Vault, Rick, was not a man who let his imagination run away with him. He was tough, businesslike and well grounded in reality. This building, however, had made Rick a believer in the paranormal. Soon after he moved his business into the building, they began to experience electrical anomalies. Lights would go on and off for no reason. The sound system would suddenly blare at full blast when no one had touched it. Doors would slam, and footsteps were heard where no one was walking.

Rick began to think about the rumors that swirled about of the previous owner. People whispered that the man had disappeared off the face of the earth, with no warning and never a sign of his existence elsewhere. There were those who suspected foul play and hinted that he had owed money to "the wrong people." Rick began to worry that the man had in fact met his end here at the bar, and perhaps his spirit remained to exact justice.

As Rick renovated the bar and back patio, he found that there were two barrels buried out back used as grease traps. Yet as he dug his shovel down into the dirt striking the top of one of the barrels, he considered the possibility that the remains of the previous owner could be inside. To be certain, he hired someone to come out and drain the barrels and inspect the interior. He was somewhat relieved to find there was no body in the barrels.

Over the years, the activity became such a regular occurrence that Rick named the ghost. LC said that one night he went down into the basement to bring up another keg of beer and heard Rick in his office counting coin change and saw the shadow of his feet walking by the bottom of the closed door. He didn't think anything of it until he went back upstairs and Rick was at the bar. "Rick, who is in your office" LC asked. "Don't worry. It's just Ivan the Hungarian Ghost!" Rick playfully replied. But he was serious.

He'd come to terms with the haunting and felt it friendlier to assign a name to whoever was haunting the building.

In the mid-2000s, a couple women were enjoying drinks at the bar, and one said she wanted to use the ladies' room before they left. Both went back through the hallway to the restroom, where one went in to use the facilities and the other stayed out in the hall. Suddenly, the lights in the ladies' room went out, and the woman screamed from her stall, startled at the darkness. The woman in the hallway tried to open the bathroom door but found that while there was an opening of about one inch, the door would not open further. The lady within the bathroom came out of the stall and started to tug on the main door while her friend continued to try to push it open. Despite being obviously open an inch, the door would not open any further. Other bar patrons came to the rescue and began pushing on the door to try to help the woman trapped inside. Finally, after about two long minutes, the door opened with no resistance.

Fort Collins Ghost Tours was invited to come into the Vault and tell the stories, and in mid-2010, we began to frequent the bar with our tour patrons and often stood right outside the bathroom door to tell the story of the woman who was temporarily trapped. Soon after the tours began, one of the tour guides stood before the wide-open door and told the story. Midway into the story, the door slammed shut. The tour guide realized that she may have been telling a story while a woman was in the bathroom, and the woman may have been offended at twenty people standing around the bathroom door while she was in there. An assistant tour guide took the tour to the next stop, and the lead tour guide stayed behind to apologize to the woman in the bathroom. After waiting a few minutes in the hall, she made way for another woman to enter the bathroom. She waited a few more minutes, and the woman who had just entered came back out. "Is the woman in there really upset?" the tour guide asked. "There isn't anyone in there," came the reply. The tour guide checked, and the room was empty. There were no windows or vents that would have blown the door closed, and the tour guide left perplexed.

The next night, the same guide walked up to the door to tell the story to another tour group. As soon as the story began, the door slammed shut with ferocious velocity. Stepping back, the tour guide hesitated and explained that this had happened the night before. Two of the women on the tour stepped forward and opened the door, only to find there was no one in the room.

On the third night, the tour guide brought a relative along on the tour to shore up confidence. She was a little shaken by this time and worried that the slamming door was a sign of hostility. She walked up to the door, and before she began the story, her relative said, "It's OK, there's nothing here. Just reach in and touch the open door, and you'll see it's alright." The guide reached in, and when her hand was just four inches from the door, it slammed shut, bumping her hand out of the way in its path. She narrowly missed having her fingers crushed in the doorjamb. Again, upon investigation, no one was found in the room. The guide vowed not to tell the story there again, and Fort Collins Tours no longer visits this site.

Recently, Rick sold the business to new owners, who renamed the place the Astoria. They've renovated it beautifully and offer an elegant establishment in which to enjoy a drink and a meal. One of the owners of Fort Collins Tours dropped by to welcome the new owners and to see the renovation. She asked if they had experienced anything paranormal, and they said they didn't think so. Yet one day, the gentleman owner had been in the hallway next to the ladies' room door and clapped to call his dog in from the back patio. Just as he clapped, the door closed by itself. He spent quite a while by the door trying to get it to do it again, but to no avail.

In the first two weeks of February 2012, the new owners and employees experienced a series of paranormal events that led them to ask us if those weeks had any significance. Their chef saw a man in the basement who turned a corner and disappeared into thin air. The mirror in the ladies' room shook violently one night for no reason. A pair of well-anchored paintings turned at a 180-degree angle with no earthly help.

An investigation of the haunting in the early morning hours yielded some stunning EVPs. Someone is heard whistling a tune in the recording, even though those investigating were not whistling. This odd phenomenon has also been experienced over in Walrus Ice Cream about a block away.

We have no explanation for the outbreak of activity, but we are once again taking tours to visit this beautiful and haunted establishment.

Starbucks: An Odd Encounter with a Victorian-Era Woman

172 North College Avenue

Starbucks seems an unlikely place for a ghost. It's modern and full of the warming scent of freshly ground coffee. Students sit at tables downing black coffee and writing papers for college classes, and older folks lounge in the overstuffed chairs, sipping lattes. But the Starbucks on North College is tucked in a corner underneath the old Northern Hotel, occupying space that has at times been a drugstore, a disco and, in much earlier times, the old Agricultural Hotel. We've gotten a fairly good description of the woman who appears at the counter at Starbucks, and we have a hunch she could be the "Founding Mother of Fort Collins."

Back in the 1800s, the first woman of European descent to settle in Fort Collins was Elizabeth Stone. She was a pioneer woman to the core, and she and her husband moved to Denver from Minnesota in a Conestoga wagon pulled by milk cows.

In 1864, the Stones moved to Fort Collins at the urging of friends to organize a mess hall for the soldiers of Camp Collins. Elizabeth sold baked goods to the soldiers and was soon fondly called "Auntie Stone," a nickname that has survived over 150 years of history.

Widowed in 1866, Auntie Stone remained in Fort Collins and embarked on a series of "firsts," including becoming the first European-descended female landowner and the first midwife in the area; she implemented the first brick kiln in northern Colorado (in partnership with H.C. Peterson), and she built and lived in the first brick house in Fort Collins. The astounding thing about all of these "firsts" and her many other accomplishments over the years was that when she came to Fort Collins, she was already in her sixties.

She also owned several businesses along the way, including a hotel and boardinghouse.

When the Stones first came to Fort Collins, they lived in a small cabin. Auntie Stone's original cabin has been moved a few times, but near the turn of the nineteenth century, it stood as a kitchen behind the Agricultural Hotel, later the Commercial Hotel and finally the Northern.

Now, in modern-day Fort Collins, Starbucks employees report that a woman in Victorian dress has been known to walk up to the counter and quietly stare past the barista. When the barista asks if he or she can help her, she slowly fades away.

It wouldn't surprise us at all to learn that this was Auntie Stone looking for a new entrepreneurial enterprise.

If you'd like to see Auntie Stone's original cabin, it has once again been moved and stands outside the old Carnegie Library at 200 Matthews Street.

ARMADILLO RESTAURANT: A LYNCHING IN LARIMER COUNTY

Why an Abusive Husband's Ghost Haunts a Local Restaurant, 354 Walnut Street

Located at the corner of Mountain and Walnut Streets stands the site of some of the most grisly and troubling history ever to haunt Fort Collins. The current occupant of the site, the Armadillo Restaurant, resonates with spectral bodies striving to tell their stories. Or perhaps they are trying to frighten those who dare to enter this certainly cursed property.

The first incident of violent death occurred in 1888 and resulted in the first and only lynching ever to take place in Larimer County.

The story of James and Eva Howe began in a home situated where the Armadillo Restaurant now stands. James and Eva married when she was only fifteen and he was considerably older. By all accounts, James was a strapping man of six-foot-four, and Eva was a diminutive young woman, sweet and shy. They lived in several places but in the 1880s settled in Fort Collins, where they moved in respectable social circles. Eva was well liked by everyone. She had a sunny and warm personality, and she was quick to volunteer when charities or those stumbling upon troubled times needed her help. She was delighted when, after many years of marriage, she and James welcomed a beloved baby daughter into their home. It seemed life was all she had hoped for.

Soon after the birth of their daughter, though, James began drinking, and he was an angry and hostile drunk. As the years passed, James's drinking worsened and with it his temper. As he descended into his nightly binges, he began violently abusing Eva. She hid the bruises under long sleeves and fashionable veils and told no one. Perhaps she was afraid of the shame and stigma it would bring to their family. Or maybe she was afraid that the law couldn't protect her from such a violent man. She silently bore the wrath of his rage, cowering each evening as he backed her into corners with his fists.

On April 3, 1888, James once again came home drunk, but this night was different. He stumbled through the front door, and Eva cringed at the smell of his liquored breath and the wild, rage-filled look in his eyes. He began his nightly ritual of punching and kicking her, but tonight he was even more brutal in his attack, and during the ordeal, he threatened to kill her. As she lay on the bedroom floor, he stood over her screaming and kicking her ribs until the pain made her pass out. When she awoke, she found James in a drunken stupor on their bed. Terrified, Eva crawled out of their room, careful not to wake her tormentor. She then crouched in the kitchen and whispered into the phone for the operator to send the police.

The police arrived within a few minutes. They dragged James from his bed, out of his room and toward the front door. Beating a woman was not a crime the civilized men of Fort Collins took lightly, and it was clear they would ensure justice for Eva. However, Eva would not press charges or allow the police to incarcerate her husband. Was she more afraid of social stigma than death? The undersheriff explained to Eva that if they didn't take James with them, she would have no protection once they left. They would not be able to guarantee her safety. She refused to press charges, and the police were forced to leave without James. Still intoxicated, James fell back onto his bed and passed out for the night.

The next morning, James awoke, and Eva made his breakfast. Both acted like the violence of the previous night had never happened. It could be that James, in his drunken blackout, didn't even remember the visit from the police. After James left for work, Eva took their five-year-old daughter over to the neighbor's house to stay for a few hours. She walked back home, pulled out her old steamer trunk and began to pack. She knew the time had come to escape. She and her daughter would be on the next train for her parents' house if all went as planned. She quickly threw clothes and other necessities into the trunk but couldn't help glancing out the front window in fear, hoping against hope that James would work all day as he usually did.

At noon, Eva's worst nightmare came true. James walked through the front door unexpectedly and saw the packed steamer trunk. There is no way to know what happened inside their home during the next few minutes. At 12:15 p.m., however, Eva stumbled out her front door and into the yard, only to be overcome by James.

James was holding a knife, and Eva was already bleeding profusely from a neck wound. She fell to her hands and knees in the front yard, and James stood over her, with his arm wrapped around her waist, first nicking her cruelly in the right side of the face with the knife and then changing hands and slitting her throat on the left side. James then turned, walked back into the house and lay down on their bed, where he was found when the authorities arrived.

Eva, still bleeding profusely, struggled to her feet one last time and, in a muffled voice, cried, "Murder!" She staggered out into the street, turned right and tried to move toward the police station a block away. She only made it as far as the edge of her own fence, where she collapsed and died.

Passersby stopped to help, but it was too late. An early arrival on the scene, a Mr. Evans, had cried for help when he saw Eva burst forth from the front door, but the winds were extremely strong that day, and his cries went unheard.

James was immediately taken into custody by law enforcement and offered no resistance. Undersheriff Stultz ushered James to the jail, followed by an entourage of townspeople threatening vengeance on James. Rather than express remorse over the death of his wife, James cried and shook and begged for his own mercy. "Please don't lynch me," he chanted over and over again between sobs. Stultz, even while under pressure from the gathering crowd amassing behind them as they made their way to the jail, assured James that lynching was not legal in Larimer County and that he would go before a judge who would determine his fate.

That afternoon, a strange and eerie quiet descended on the town. There were few people on the streets and even fewer horses and carriages out than usual. However, in the back alleys and saloons, groups of local men met, talking in hushed voices, while other townspeople gathered outside the jail to harass the murderer.

At eight o'clock that evening all of the lights to the city of Fort Collins were mysteriously cut, and the city fell into complete and utter darkness. Bands of men, all wearing masks, approached the jail from several directions. Not a word was spoken as the bands arrived almost simultaneously at the jail.

The mobs held the undersheriff and his deputy at gunpoint, but Stultz refused to give up the keys to James Howe's cell. James's cell was under heavy lock and bolt, and the mob was forced to break through the bolt with chisel and hammer, which took nearly half an hour. Throughout this process, James cowered in the back corner of his cell, shaking and begging not to be lynched, clearly and justifiably terrified of the angry mob. Once the lock was broken, James was dragged from his cell, whimpering and crying for mercy. Still shaking with fear, he was dragged down an alley and over to a crane, where a rope had been hung. When asked if he had any last words, he said he had a brother and sister in Kansas and again begged for mercy. The noose was placed around his neck, and his hands and feet were bound. Masked men pulled the other end of the rope over the crane. James's pitiful screams were cut short as he was hoisted by his neck up into the air, and after a few tortured moments, his body went limp.

Following his demise, the crowd dispersed in an eerily quiet and orderly manner. The undersheriff and coroner arrived on the scene about an hour later to cut him down and take him to the morgue.

In a strange postscript to this story, rumor has it that Eva and James were buried side by side in Grandview Cemetery. Don't go looking for their graves, though. For some reason, no headstones were ever erected, although the family could well afford them. Why they were not identified is a mystery to this day.

This would have been the end of the story if James, Eva and their daughter had faded into the history books without reappearing in ghostly form.

Many years later, the old Howe home moved to another location in Fort Collins, and a new building was erected on the site. In 1975, the building was purchased and has since been home to the Armadillo Restaurant.

Employees and patrons of the Armadillo have reported a very tall, hostile, ghostly presence hanging out at the end of the bar (James's favorite spot in his earthly life) and in the kitchen. One employee reported a tall man walking down the hall from the restaurant to the bar toward her, and as he got closer, she noticed he was walking with his feet about one foot off the ground. He then disappeared. Another employee was so startled by a male apparition in the kitchen glaring at her in a threatening manner that she walked out, quit and never returned.

Women have reported disturbing sights in the ladies' restroom. A small girl (perhaps five years old or so) has been seen sitting on the changing table. As the girl turns toward the onlooker, it becomes apparent she has no eyes. Other customers have come out of the restroom looking ashen and shaken and reported a diminutive woman in the restroom wearing a white linen nightgown. They say she is bleeding from her cheek and her neck and that her nightgown is covered in blood.

Interestingly, most of the sightings come from people who have never heard of James or Eva Howe and certainly have no knowledge of their sad and violent ends. Could it be that James and Eva still walk the halls of their old home, replaying that sordid last day? And what about their daughter, who went to live with her grandparents but suffered the trauma of her parents' murders—does she hover there, too, trying to make sense of it all but unable to truly see how this could happen?

But James and Eva are not the only ghosts who haunt this tragic place, nor is this the only story of violent deaths on the property. For more about the hauntings of the Armadillo Restaurant, read on.

ARMADILLO GARAGE: A CURSED PROPERTY?

354 Walnut Street

There are places where a tragedy has befallen the people who dwell there, and as a result, there is a haunting. There are places where more than one tragedy has occurred, and we call those places "unfortunate." But when a particular piece of property has seen a murder and multiple suicides and hosted the remains of a disaster, we call it cursed. The site where the Armadillo Restaurant stands is just such a place.

We don't know what this property was used for prior to European settlement in the 1860s. We can only speculate that it was traversed by the Sioux, Arapahoe and Cheyenne tribes that frequented the area. Perhaps the French fur traders stopped there on their journeys to the Rockies and prepared for trapping expeditions. In any case, we will always wonder if some terrible curse was cast upon this land, as it has been the scene of unspeakable and consistent sadness and tragedy since Fort Collins history has been recorded.

The first tragedy recorded is recounted in the previous section. In April 1883, after continual abuse, Eva Howe was murdered by her husband, James, on this site. Witnessed by passersby on Walnut Street, James slit Eva's throat in broad daylight in their front yard. She managed to rise to her feet and stagger toward the street, trying to mouth "Murder!" but her words were carried off in the strong wind of the Front Range.

Eighty years later, in the early 1960s, that property had become a car dealership. Brand-new Ramblers were parked on display inside the showroom. Salesman dressed in dark trousers, white shirts and thin black

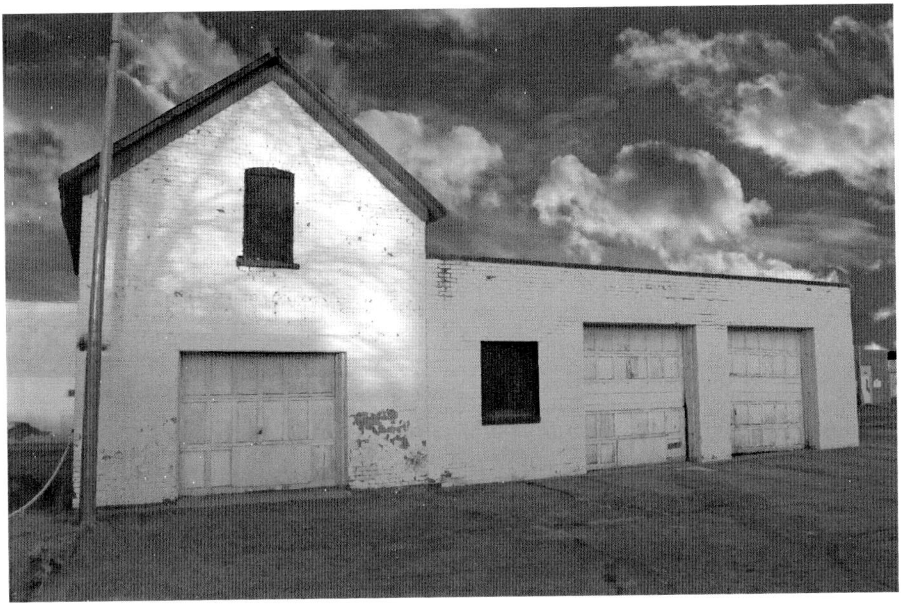

The Armadillo Garage (old AMC dealership).

ties took customers on test drives and urged them to buy the "car of their dreams." Being a car salesman was a high-pressure job. A good salesman could make good money. Those who didn't sell their quota often found themselves in financial trouble.

We don't know why the following tragedy happened; we have only the hearsay of old-timers who have lived in Fort Collins for decades. They tell us that one early morning before the dealership opened, a salesman let himself into the dealership and walked into the showroom full of shiny new cars. He threw a rope over one of the beams in the showroom, fashioned a noose and hanged himself. When the general manager opened up the showroom in the morning, he was greeted with the grisly scene of his salesman swinging above the cars. We will probably never know what drove this poor man to end his life, but we do know he haunts that building. Employees and customers of the Armadillo Restaurant have seen the man dressed in dark trousers, white shirt and thin black tie walking across the main room of the restaurant (presumably where the showroom would have been fifty years ago). He walks with a sense of purpose and pays no attention to those around him. Many have seen his apparition and thought he was one of the employees, only to see him disappear before their eyes as he walked by.

In the early 1980's, many buildings in Old Town had fallen into a state of disrepair and abandonment. New development to the south of the area had driven commerce away from this once-thriving downtown, and it became a sad ghost of the town it had been in its heyday. The site and building at the corner of Walnut and Mountain sat vacant and alone. Teenage vandals, homeless and others down on their luck were the only ones to show any interest in the buildings that stood waiting for revival. However, one man had a dream for the property at Mountain and Walnut. He stood in the parking lot and looked to the right at the old dealership building and then toward the back at what had been the repair garage.

The garage was older and had been built with a roof pitch that made it look a bit more like a home than a commercial building. Many windows had been broken, and the two large rooms inside were visible from the parking lot. For some reason, there were also smaller rooms built around corners in the garage, giving one the feeling that something could jump out at them at any time.

The man strolled around the property and began to make plans. Rather than the decrepit and sad buildings that stood before him, the man saw the potential for a thriving restaurant. He was an experienced businessman, and he knew potential when he saw it. He walked to his car, resolved to purchase this property. He still owns it today.

Shortly after the man purchased the property, he drove over to once again check out the buildings. What he found in the garage first made his blood run cold and then cast a pall of sadness over the property for many years to come.

Three days before this visit, another young man, only nineteen years old and devastated for reasons we will never know, broke into the garage. He carried with him a shotgun and a sadness that brought him to only one final conclusion: he would take his own life. He stood in the middle of the smaller garage room, pointed the shotgun at his head and pulled the trigger. Nothing happened. The trigger jammed, and the gun was rendered useless. The young man was still determined to end his life. He pulled his car into the garage and yanked down the garage door. He climbed into the front seat and started the car. Sometime during the night, the exhaust fumes ended his young life. He was not found for several days, when the new owner came to view his new property.

Employees of the Armadillo have reported hearing things and seeing things in the garage that can't be explained. They don't like to even set foot in the garage. When Fort Collins Tours heard rumors of the garage being haunted, we asked if we might take tours into the garage. The manager agreed and invited us over to get the key. When we picked up the key on a sunny June morning, we asked if an employee would come out to the garage and show us around. No one volunteered. After speaking with a total of eleven employees, we've heard story after story about the hauntings of both the restaurant and the garage, but there is something about the garage that particularly frightens and repels them. It's a feeling more than anything, heavy and sickening, enveloping some when they walk into the garage. We've noted that people on our tours sometimes experience this and become so ill they have to leave.

Last September, a gentleman on our tour came to us during our presentation in the garage and asked if we knew what the garage had been used for in 1951. His story led us to more history and a bit of a mystery.

The gentleman was clearly into his eighties, with a shock of white hair and a spry gait. He had been with the area search and rescue operations in the 1940s and '50s and had seen firsthand much of the history of our town. He told us that in 1951, the seventh worst commercial aviation disaster in American history happened right here in Fort Collins. A plane carrying fifty people—forty-five passengers and five crew members—had gone down on Crystal Mountain just west of Fort Collins. The plane was en route from San Francisco to Chicago via Denver. Somehow the pilot had made an error in navigation (according to the flight commission) and routed the plane into a mountainous area where it should never have been. The crash was fiery and left a skid mark of many hundreds of feet as it careened across the land. Search and rescue crews rushed to the remote site, but there were no survivors.

Rather than a rescue effort, the search and rescue crew embarked on a mission to identify the victims and contact their families. Bodies were taken to the morgue, and the plane seats were taken to the garage at the Armadillo to be stored until further investigation of the incident was completed.

Over the years, memory of this flight faded away, and by 2011, there were very few people in the community who had even heard of it. What happened during one of our tours, therefore, was rather stunning regarding an otherworldly communication with great specificity of details.

Now and then we have someone along on the tour who brings his or her own equipment. On one of our tours last summer, we had a young teenager who brought an application that gathers energy from the area and basically emits words through the application on an iPhone. Initially, we weren't too interested in the app. How effective and "real" could it be for a $1.99 app on an iPhone?

The young man turned it on in the garage, and the following words immediately emanated from his iPhone: "fly," "explode," "metal," "hijack" and "suppress." Stunned, I made note of the words and downloaded the app while we were still on the tour in the garage. Mine came out with the words "Korea" and "atom," which I debunked as being just random words that didn't have any relationship to the plane crash.

We began to research the crash and initiated contact with the late pilot's daughter. She had done extensive research on the crash and had even written a book about it. She was convinced that there was more to the crash than the Federal Aviation Administration (FAA) had released.

The official cause of the crash had been listed as pilot error, but she shared with us that her father was an experienced pilot who had made that flight regularly. He would never have made the navigational error the FAA said he did. Further, the FAA had repeatedly refused to release the recording of the last communications and conversations with the pilot. Years later, the pilot's daughter learned that those words had to do with asking someone why he was up there in the cockpit and telling him he would have to leave. Why would someone have made his way to the cockpit, and who would the pilot have ordered out?

The pilot's daughter told us there had been a man onboard from U.S. Intelligence who had a metal briefcase handcuffed to his wrist. When the flight went down, members of U.S. Intelligence converged on the crash site, found the briefcase and brought it to a bank manager in Fort Collins. They asked him to store it in the bank vault until it could be retrieved. She later came to the conclusion from interviews and conversations with others in the intelligence field that the briefcase had probably contained atomic secrets. The crash happened during the Korean War, and there was quite a bit of atomic research being conducted. Later in her research, it was confirmed that the briefcases carried by two military couriers did indeed contain forty secret and top-secret/coded atomic items.

Was the plane brought down by a hijacker because of the secrets in the briefcase? Why did the U.S. government suppress the last conversation Captain Appleby had with the ground crew via radio transmission? These are mysteries we may never solve, but we believe someone from that era knows the answer.

In the meantime, we wonder if some of the victims whose personal items may have been stored in the Armadillo garage might have been trying to communicate with us—"fly," "explode," "metal," "suppress" and "hijack" all seem to be too much of a coincidence to ignore. And "Korea" and "atom," which I dismissed at the time, made perfect sense after hearing the daughter's story. In a later investigation of the garage, one of the words emitted by the phone app was "crystal." The plane went down on Crystal Mountain. Are these folks trying to communicate from beyond what really happened on that fateful flight?

We've had ongoing paranormal experiences at this garage that indicate a desire for communication.

After one of our Midnight Ghost Tours, a few tour participants went back to the Armadillo Garage to explore the exterior. One of them, an amateur ghost hunter, thumped on the side door in the old percussive pattern—*bump, ba-da bump, bump*—and waited, only to hear the responsive *bump bump* immediately after from the inside of the door. Curious to see if there was, in fact, someone in the building, another person from the group peered in the window. There was no one there, but they clearly heard someone just on the other side of the window growl, "Get the ----away from here!" This garage is locked up tight, and there is no alternate way in. The owners have gone to some trouble to secure the building, as it had been a draw for vagrants decades ago, so it was not very likely there would be a human being in the garage in the early morning hours.

On several occasions, people on the tour have seen the apparition of a man in the very back room of the garage, and he disappears quickly. Twice, tour-goers have taken digital pictures only to find the image of a man's face in front of the item they were photographing.

One night, in the back storage room, a woman on the tour jumped and said it felt like someone was blowing on her neck. We had an amateur ghost-hunting team with us that night, and they walked over to her with an EMF meter and a thermometer. The area next to her was several degrees colder (twenty plus), and the EMF meter was off the charts, despite the fact that there is no electrical power in this building at all. The team followed the cold spot around the garage with the thermometer and the EMF for almost five minutes before the activity dissipated.

The Armadillo Garage has become one of our most "active" spots on the tour, and we often experience some type of paranormal activity during the tours. From cold spots to high EMF readings and pictures of apparitions, this site has proven it is worthy of mention in both paranormal and historical collections.

Postscript: Wreckage of the plane still exists up on Crystal Mountain. Heavy equipment was brought in to cover it with dirt, but over the last sixty or so years, the earth has eroded, and the plane parts are once again visible. A man on one of our recent tours had been up there in the last few months and shared that it's still a sobering scene. It isn't easy to find or to access. One would need a guide from the area to get there.

THE VIRGIN OF GUADALUPE AND THE ARMADILLO

In February 2012, we received a call from the manager of the Armadillo Restaurant asking us if we would come by and see something of interest. I hung up the phone and walked the three blocks down to the Armadillo.

When I arrived, the manager led me to the bar, which has an expanse of windows facing west. It was about 4:00 p.m., and the sun was setting; sunlight was streaming in through the windows. The light through one of the windows clearly depicted a Madonna-like image in the glass. The manager explained that when they first saw it, they thought it was interesting but assumed it was just the way the watermark had been left the last time the window had been washed. Just for fun, he took a picture of it. Amazingly, in the picture the watermark had within it the darker picture of a woman with a black scarf over her head and a very clear image of a cross on her neck.

This seemed like an incredible, one-time picture. However, when subsequent pictures were taken, others had the same image. There was absolutely nothing within the glass image that would reflect that dark photo.

One of the owners took the image to her priest, who said it looked like the image of the Virgin of Guadalupe, a woman who had experienced a virgin birth and who was revered in the Catholic Church.

The image remains and can be seen from the interior of the bar in the late afternoon and early evening just as the sun sets. Is it possible that there has been such darkness and pain cloaking this place that the Virgin of Guadalupe has appeared to bless and cleanse the area? Or is it just another piece of a puzzle in the afterlife that we just can't understand?

If you have a chance, drop by the Armadillo and ask if you can have dinner in the bar around sunset. Perhaps you will see the Madonna-like reflection in the glass or even get a picture of the Virgin of Guadalupe.

Choice City Butcher and the Haunted Butcher Block

104 West Olive Street

Poltergeists have been a subject of fascination for paranormal researchers for the last two centuries. The word *poltergeist* is German for "noisy ghost," and it is a fitting description. Poltergeists tend to make their presence known and are reputedly able to move objects, cause fires and shatter glass. One of the hallmarks of poltergeist activity is that it centers on a person or thing. These spirits tend to be attached to either a living human being, known in the paranormal world as an "agent," or to an item of personal meaning. If that person or item moves to a new location, the location will experience paranormal activity. Choice City Butcher and Deli in Old Town Fort Collins has been the host of a poltergeist ever since it opened and brought a used butcher block into the building.

Choice City Butcher and Deli is a local favorite for incredibly tasty Reuben sandwiches and a vast array of beers on tap. Located near the corner of Olive Street and College Avenue, just south of the Old Town area, it's still within the boundaries of historical district buildings and Old World charm.

Russ started this shop a few years ago on a budget. To save money, he scanned the classifieds for gently used equipment, coolers and other tools of the trade. He was excited to find an old-fashioned butcher block in one of the papers and called to get more information. The woman he spoke with described the block, and it sounded like something that would fit perfectly in his new but elegantly old-fashioned shop. Arrangements were made for him to view the butcher block in a storage area in the neighboring town of Greeley.

When Russ arrived at the storage area, he parked the car and knocked on the storage door. He was surprised to find the woman in tears. "I'm so sorry I had you come all the way over here!" she said. "I can't part with this butcher block. I thought I could, but it belonged to my dad and he just passed away. He worked at this block for thirty-five years, and it's a part of him. I just don't think I can sell it."

Russ nodded and assured her that he understood. They spoke for a while about his plans to open the butcher shop and his dreams for the future and then about the woman's father and how he had loved being in the same business. When Russ went to leave, he turned to her and said, "If you ever

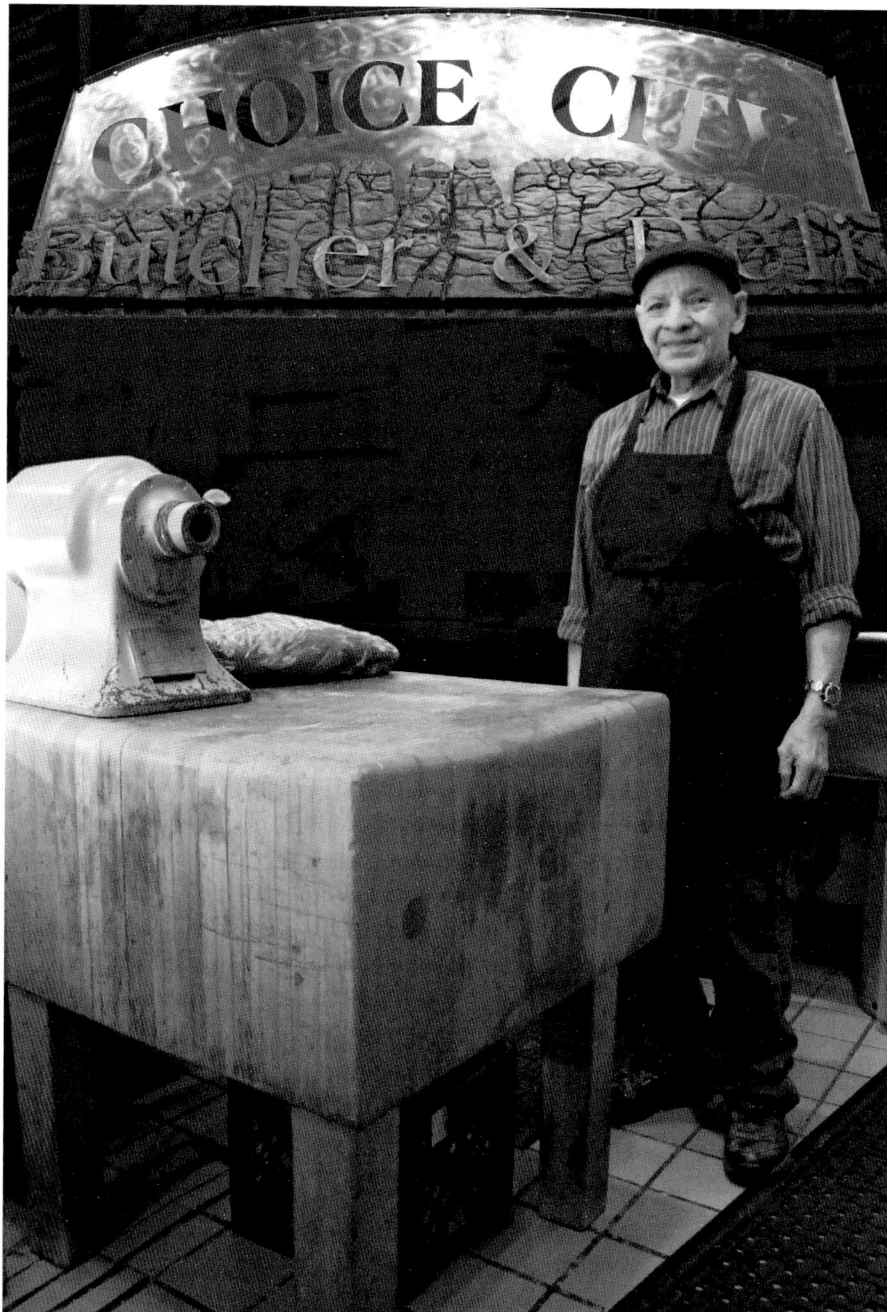

Choice City Butcher.

change your mind, give me a call. If you ever decide to sell the butcher block, I'll respect it and what it meant to your dad, and if I ever close the shop, I'd give it back to you."

As he walked to the car, he heard the storage door open again. She called out, "Wait! My dad would have liked you, and he would have wanted to see a young man starting in the business using his butcher block. I will sell it to you!" Russ paid her, loaded the block into his truck and brought it back to the shop.

The butcher block was lovingly installed near the back of the shop, and Russ and his hired butcher began to use it immediately. Within weeks, the second butcher soon began seeing a man to the left of the butcher block, just watching him work. When he turned toward him, the man would disappear. As many people would, the butcher questioned his own eyesight. Could his imagination be playing tricks on him? But over the next few months, the spectral appearances became more frequent, and they lingered long enough for the butcher to turn and see him clearly.

One afternoon, the butcher, having had a bad day, was taking out some of his frustrations on the butcher block. He raised the meat cleaver and brought it down heavily on the butcher block several times, expressing his anger. Suddenly, an entire shelf of glassware along the window at the front of the store shattered into thousands of tiny glass shards. Was this the ghostly man's way of saying, "Don't hurt my butcher block"? To this day, there is no other plausible explanation for why a dozen or so glasses would spontaneously shatter into bits.

Poltergeists do tend to come and go within a fairly short time period. The longest recorded poltergeist haunting was fifteen years. However, according to anecdotal paranormal research, they average anywhere from two months to two years. This man has haunted Choice City Butcher for over nine years. Maybe he's going for some kind of ghostly record!

Starry Night: Who Is the Lady in Pink?

112 South College Avenue

We (Fort Collins Tours) heard about the haunting in Starry Night's basement from local folks and went there to investigate. Becky, the owner of the

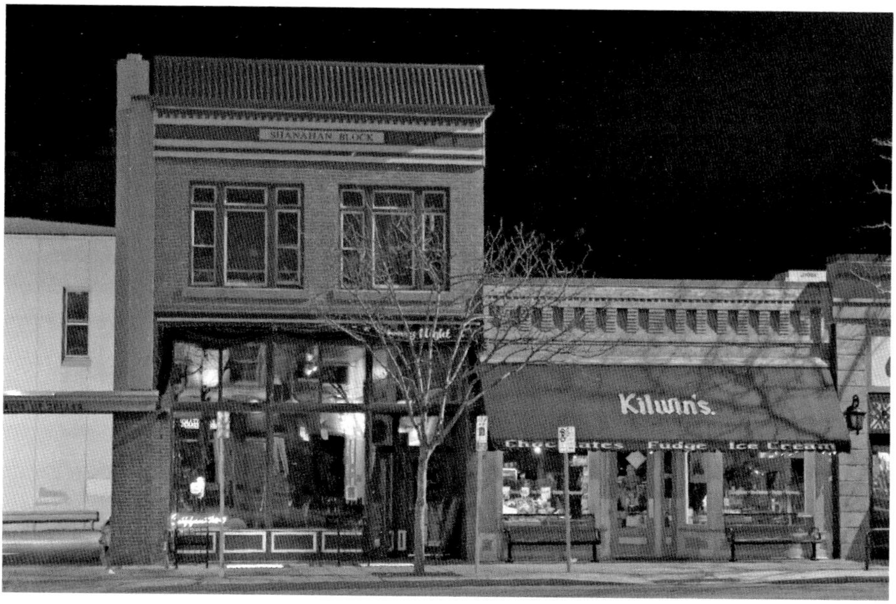

Starry Night.

charming bistro, invited us to bring tours into and under the establishment and told us that her daughter, Jennifer, had periodically seen the ghost of a young woman in a pink (almost salmon) dress in the basement.

Jennifer is an amazing chef, and she bakes incredible cakes, bars, cookies and other delectable desserts for Starry Night to sell. I often joke on tours that if the place were not already haunted, it would be as soon as I pass on, as my idea of heaven is hanging out sampling those desserts!

Jen told us that the young lady whose apparition she had seen seemed content to stay in one corner of the basement, but she would just silently stare at Jen as she worked. It was unnerving for Jen, and when it started, she felt uncomfortable in the basement. Even when she didn't see the young lady, she felt she was being watched.

We began to lead tours into the basement and often took EMF readings in the corner where Jen had reported the young lady stood. One night, the EMF spiked and continued to read at the highest level. Since there could be other sources of electricity in the basement, we didn't assume the activity was paranormal until we heard the shuffling of feet in the corner when no one was there. We had a tour of about fifteen people gathered around when this happened, and several of the tour participants started to take digital photos. Suddenly, one young girl gasped as she checked her camera. "Look at what I got!" she exclaimed. We gathered around, and there on her camera screen was a turn-of-the-century salmon pink gown. We could see the bodice and the gentle outflow of the skirt. The woman was not visible, but it was a clear photo of the dress.

Months later, we had a psychic along on a tour, and she asked if she could go ahead of the group and see if she felt anything before she heard the stories. We had not yet visited Starry Night but were at a stop prior to it. She was listening to a story about the current site when she mentioned that there was a young lady in a salmon pink dress following the tour guide around on the tour. The tour guide, startled by the description, said there was a haunting by a young lady in a salmon pink dress, but not at this stop on the tour. The psychic laughed and said, "They can move around, you know!" The tour guide shuddered, but the psychic assured her that the young lady was friendly and just wanted companionship. She was not a threat and was unlikely to follow anyone home.

On one of our recent tours, a participant took a digital photo of the same area and got the picture of a young girl's face peeking out around the corner. We wonder if it's the same young lady.

Research of that building has yielded no history that would indicate a haunting, but there was another tragedy just down the block that could explain the apparition of a shy but friendly young lady. See the Welch Block Fire story for more on this possible connection.

The Walrus Man and the Town's Most Prolific Spiritual Portal

Walrus Ice Cream Shop, 125 West Mountain Avenue

Spiritual portals are rare. They are found above bodies of water or underground rivers, and they act a bit like "revolving doors" for spirits who wish to transport back and forth between our world and theirs. Spectral activity is heightened around these portals.

In the 1870s, Miss Rose opened a millinery shop on Mountain Street in Fort Collins. She sold fancy hats, handmade scarves and fashionable

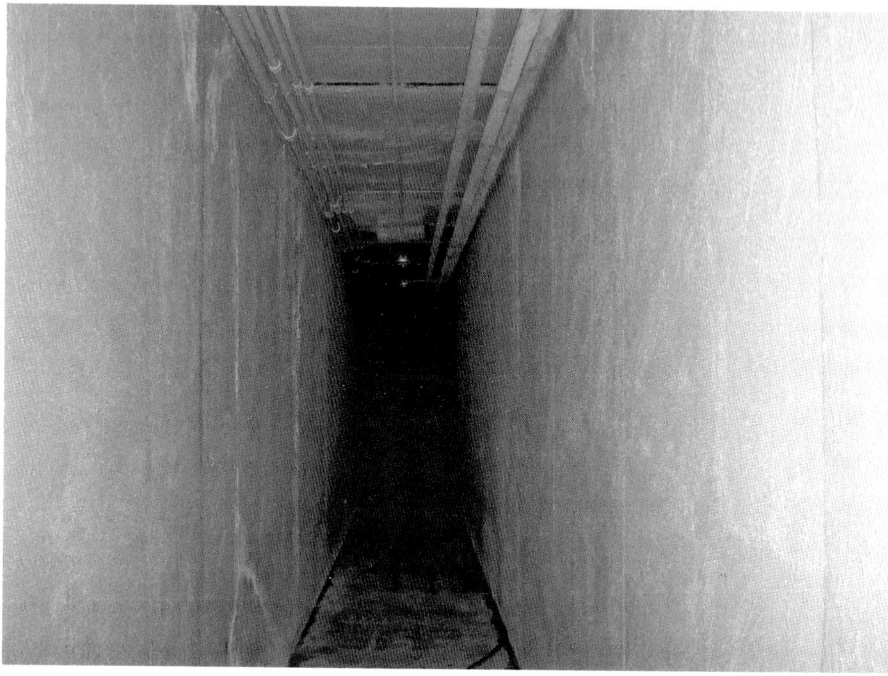

The Walrus tunnel.

handbags. Her shop was a hub of social interaction among the women of Fort Collins and, by all accounts, quite a busy establishment.

Miss Rose built her shop above a high-water table. In fact, the river could be seen running just a few feet below the basement. It seemed a strange place to build a millinery shop, but Rose had easy access to clean water running right down from the Rockies. In a day when one had to hand dig wells, this made sense.

Next door to Miss Rose's Millinery Shop stood the old morgue, mausoleum and crematorium. The morgue was a majestic building, two stories high with a basement. The stone façade and elaborate cornices gave the impression of wealth and elegance, and the interior parlor was a place of calm reflection. The basement, however, was a dark and troubled place housing the crematorium, embalming paraphernalia and other sides of this trade better left unseen.

There is no mention in museum archives or other documentation about this morgue or the stories surrounding it, but oral histories collected by those whose parents walked the streets of Fort Collins around the turn of

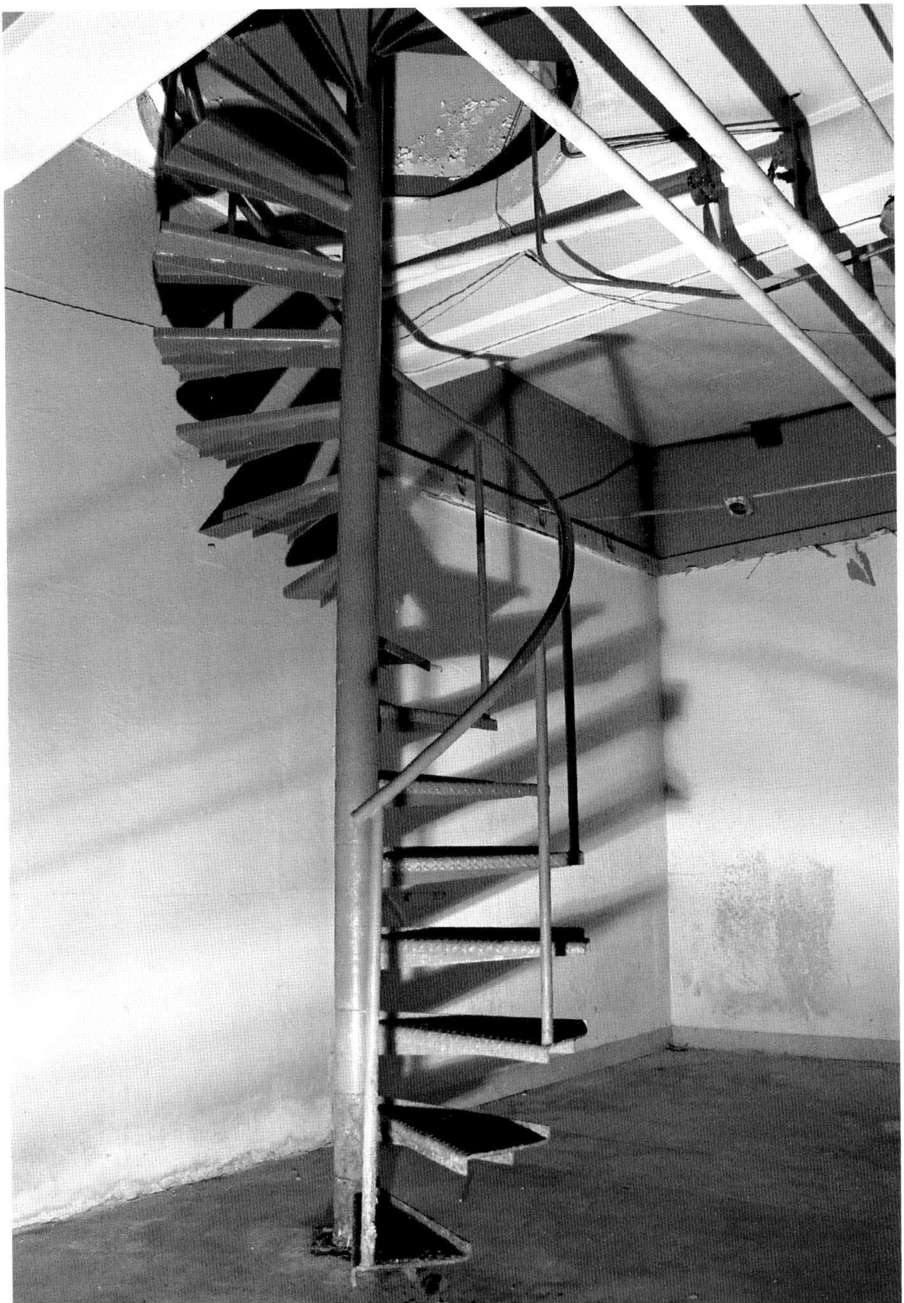

The Walrus staircase.

the century shed light on the activities and people surrounding this little diorama that led to such a haunted site.

According to many accounts, there was a ramp that went down underneath the millinery shop, where horse-and-carriage hearses could go underground to drop off bodies and pick up caskets with remains going to the cemetery. There was an arched entrance from the basement of the morgue leading out to the hearse bay underneath the back lot behind the millinery shop. This bay was covered by a wooden platform, so the entire exchange of bodies was made out of sight of the general public. It wasn't considered good taste or good business to load and unload human remains in the light of the day.

More than a century later, the morgue had become a Mexican restaurant, and the millinery shop had been replaced by the Walrus Ice Cream Shop on the front of the property and above the river. A parking lot sits behind the ice cream shop, and underneath the parking lot stretches a long tunnel leading to a huge underground room. The origins of this tunnel and many tunnels throughout the Old Town area are unknown.

A few years ago, a local intuitive, Kim Pentecost, identified a spiritual portal in one of these underground rooms—the one with a view of the river running underneath. She said that it was a spectral hub where spirits made their way in and out of their world and into Old Town. While there is no scientific way to verify such a claim, there is ample anecdotal evidence that Kim may have indeed found a portal.

Employees of the Walrus Ice Cream Shop have continually reported hearing voices down in the basement rooms and tunnel, and one young lady said an unseen hand had grabbed her ankle. Almost all the employees were afraid to visit the basement alone.

Fort Collins Tours began taking groups down into the basement rooms and the tunnel in May 2011. In the minds of the tour guides, it was another fun and interesting stop filled with the history and mystery of old Fort Collins. It wasn't long, however, before the guides began to wonder if this was a stop better left off the tour.

During some of the first tours, the guests frequently reported being tapped on the right shoulder when no one was anywhere near them. Young ladies often were startled by the sensation of a cold hand gripping one of their ankles. Women had their hair pulled, particularly after expressing disbelief.

One of the tour experiences is taking an EVP while we are in a large room at the end of a fairly long, dark tunnel. A digital voice recorder is activated, and the group remains absolutely silent. When the recording is played back, the theory is that there will be only silence. If there is a voice on the recorder, it could be ghostly communication.

In June 2011, we had seventeen tour guests and three tour guides in the large room, and we prepared to take an EVP. We noticed that the electromagnetic field meter (EMF), a device used for measuring energy in the area, was recording higher energy readings than normal, and since it beeps when this occurs, we turned it off to do the EVP recording. We asked all to be silent and still for fifteen to twenty seconds, and we stood in the dark, recording nothing but the sound of occasional dripping water from the ancient ceiling into puddles on the ground.

Twenty seconds passed. "Is everyone ready to hear what we recorded?" the guide asked. All nodded in agreement. The recording played back, and a ghostly whisper was clearly heard, although no one could make out what it said. Unfortunately, this was a little too much for some of the tour guests. One woman started to cry, and a number of the guests started for the tunnel entrance even though it was too dark to leave without the guides and flashlights.

Later in the month, the recording of the voice was given to a local radio DJ to enhance and isolate in order to discern what was said. Although the voice became very clear, we still couldn't make out any words.

We continued to play the EVP for subsequent tour groups and kept taking new EVPs with each group, although none reflected another voice. Interestingly enough, every time we played the EVP with the man's voice, the EMF meter would flash and beep, as if to say, "That's me talking!" Late in the summer, we played the EVP for the group, and a woman said, "I know why you couldn't make out the words—he's speaking French!" This woman, a French instructor at the local college, translated it for us. "This isn't my daughter" or "This isn't my girl" are the two possible translations for the single sentence recorded.

We wondered if the gentleman speaking was looking for a particular woman and if that was why he continually tapped shoulders, grabbed ankles and pulled the hair of our female tour guests.

On a late night in August 2011, one of our tour guides was closing up the room with the spiritual portal. RJ is six feet, three inches tall and in his mid-twenties and had been pretty skeptical of the idea of real ghosts. He viewed the tours as entertainment, though, and enjoyed leading them. On this particular night, he checked the room to ensure no one had lagged behind and stepped out into the hallway. He began to pull the door closed when a dark, spectral man taller than him peeked out around the door at him as it closed. He recounts doing what any big, strong, well-grounded man would do—he ran down the hall, up the stairs and into the well-lit ice cream shop! Unsure of what he had seen and in fear that people would think he was crazy, he kept his encounter to himself for the next couple weeks.

Another tour guide, an older woman, was closing up the same room a couple weeks later and saw a man in the middle of the room standing about six feet, four inches tall. Thinking it was RJ, she exclaimed, "You scared me, don't do that!" At that moment, the figure disappeared before her eyes! She hurried down the hall to the room where RJ and the rest of the group were starting back up to the ground level and whispered to RJ about what she had seen. At that point, he told her about his experience.

Another two weeks passed, and a third guide, CJ, was down in the basement unlocking doors and preparing for a tour to visit. He heard footsteps back by the portal room and immediately assumed it was one of the ice cream shop employees. In an effort not to startle them, he called, "Tour guide coming through!" and made his way down the hall to the room. When he arrived, he found no one there. CJ shrugged and decided he'd heard an echo of his own footsteps. He entered a side room and then again heard footsteps in the hallway. He came to the doorway and listened as spectral footsteps walked right past him with no visible person attached to them and turned into the room where the apparition had been seen.

In the fall of 2011, the tour was visited by a local psychic. Robbin has a good reputation and does not charge for her services. She asked if she could visit the sites just a few moments before the tour guide began to tell the stories so she could "read" the area and let another tour participant know what she saw. At each stop, she told other tour guests (none of whom she knew) what she experienced, and she was incredibly accurate, often offering details of activity we hadn't shared with guests on previous tours.

When we reached the basement with the portal room, she reported meeting a tall, thin man with a goatee. He spoke both French and English. His first words to her were: "Where's CJ?" CJ wasn't on this tour and hadn't been guiding for a couple months. Robbin would have had no way of knowing that there even was a guide named CJ.

We called CJ to tell him about our spectral visitor asking for him. He had heard all the stories about the Walrus, maybe dozens of times as he tagged along on tours. He had even had his own encounters with the presence we referred to as the Walrus Man. None of us really believed there was anything malicious about this playful spirit; however, being in the presence of something as strange and unfamiliar as a ghost can still be a terrifying experience under the right circumstances.

CJ was a busy engineer who often traveled throughout the United States supporting various projects for a military contractor. His role as a part owner of Fort Collins Tours was limited as it related to the ghost tours; however, he often came along to help out or to collect pictures for various online and print media.

One night on the tour, he was setting up two specialized cameras on tripods in the large room at the end of the tunnel under Walrus Ice Cream. Often, he would go down ahead of the tour to set up, but at this time the entire tour party was in the center of the room listening to the tour guide tell stories about the haunted site. CJ was in the back left corner near one of the spiral staircases that led up to an abandoned bank teller nest. We were all aware of the special nature of this corner. There had been numerous occasions of unexplained EMF activity, temperature fluctuations and other strange occurrences.

CJ positioned a camera equipped with infrared night vision capability against the back wall to take pictures parallel to the sidewall leading toward the tunnel. With CJ behind the camera and his back facing the far wall, his right side was only a couple feet from the staircase. The tour group was only twenty-five feet or so away from CJ in the center of the room, but he was alone (more or less) in the dark corner.

As he positioned his eye into the eyecup of the camera and focused on adjusting various settings for optimal image quality in near darkness, somebody grabbed the material on the right arm of his jacket and gently tugged on it twice toward the staircase. He was a little startled at first, but there was not a reason for fear since the motion seemed intended to just get his attention. He pulled back quickly from the camera; however, he was slightly blinded by the camera-illuminated projection in his right eye while he was adjusting the night vision camera. Looking through just his left eye, he peered into the dark corner with the spiral staircase. There was just enough room to move around the staircase and not much way to get around CJ or his camera equipment. It was also unlikely that someone could quietly and quickly sneak away from the corner without him noticing, so he thought to himself that the individual must still be there.

He continued to peer into the corner as his eyes began to adjust to what little light there was. Expecting to see a snickering prankster in the corner, he was not amused at what he thought was a childish prank. But he was a little more cautious than he would normally be. After all, he had encounters with the Walrus Man before—albeit, this would be the first time physical contact was made. Furthermore, others had told numerous similar stories about this large dark room under the city.

He reached slowly into the darkness and moved toward the corner to where he could finally see everything. However, there was nobody there to be seen. His next thoughts were doubt and how ridiculous he must seem to any of the tour attendees who were now done with the story and starting to explore the room a little more on their own. CJ looked around quickly one more time from side to side, hoping to see someone—anyone—who could have tugged on his jacket. By this time, the closest living soul to him was one of the tour attendees about fifteen feet away.

CJ turned back to the corner and shook his head. In any normal circumstance, he would have just forgotten about the experience and certainly would not have told anybody. But this was the Fort Collins Ghost Tour. In a strange way, this was why he was in this dark and forbidding place. He had mixed feelings of anxiousness and satisfaction. He was also more anxious to be sure to leave with the group than at any other time in the past when he was on the tour. He quickly packed up the equipment and followed the tour group as it left.

That corner became a hotbed of activity on tours. Tour guests have snapped photos of tubes of light descending the spiral staircase. A warm spot in midair when the rest of the room measured a temperature of thirty-two degrees Fahrenheit was felt by a group of tour guests for five to seven minutes, and again, the EMF was off the charts in this one area.

We don't know who the tall Frenchman is, but we can only speculate that he might have been one of the French fur traders who helped found our community. The first Europeans in the area were hardy men who braved the harsh elements and rugged terrain to make their fortunes in fur trapping during the early 1800s. Perhaps our "Walrus Man" loved the area so much that he decided to make it his eternal home!

Jilly Bean Java: Mother and Children Haunt the Old Underground Morgue

240 Walnut Street

No one enjoying a hot cup of coffee while lounging in an overstuffed chair in Jilly Bean Java would suspect she is sitting atop an underground jail morgue. Jilly's is one of those great college town haunts, full of students with laptops, musicians waiting for open-mic night and locals who know where to get the world's best hot chocolate. The coffee house "regulars," however, are familiar with the sounds of a ghostly mother and children running around the hardwood floors and the presence of a man who lurks in the basement.

The morgue was part of the old jail built in 1879. Many of the Old West jails were built underground, possibly to contain pestilence and disease, which often took the lives of the prisoners who were stacked in close quarters. The Fort Collins jail contained a makeshift morgue, also underground, so it's no surprise that the present upstairs tenant, Jilly's, is haunted. However, it is puzzling that the spirits that haunt Jilly's appear to be a woman and her children when the majority of the old jail inmates would have been men.

When Jillian started Jilly's in the late summer of 2010, she frequently heard the sounds of a woman and children running around the hardwood floors and talking and laughing. Employees heard them, too, and also reported that coffee filters, plastic silverware and other items would fly off the counters from time to time, with no wind or other movement to propel them.

Jillian smudged with sage to clear the space (this is a traditional "cure"), and it seemed to quiet the spirits. However, in the spring of 2011, Jillian allowed Fort Collins Tours to bring its ghost tours in to talk about the hauntings, and activity started up again. It's a well-known belief in paranormal studies that if you go looking for ghosts, they'll come looking for you, and this has certainly been the case. Shortly after the tours began descending the steep, narrow stairs into the sandstone and dirt basement where the morgue had been, spectral activity resumed.

In June 2011, tour patrons were snapping digital photos down in the old morgue. One photo reflected the haunting image of a little boy over in a corner. Four months later, in the same spot, another tour patron captured a photo of the same little boy in a different position.

Up in the coffeehouse during the summer of 2011, Jillian and several of her regulars were going about their business when a photo on the wall came out from the wall about a foot and fell to the ground, completely avoiding anything below that would normally have become collateral damage from the falling action. This is a common theme among businesses in this block—photos and artwork tend to come off the wall about a foot before falling, as if to verify that something out of the ordinary is afoot.

Later in the summer (again in a coffeehouse full of customers, employees and a coffee company representative), a large cardboard sign sitting atop an oversized stainless steel refrigerator began to slowly slither toward the front of the shop. It slid about four feet over the top of the fridge before falling over the edge and onto the hardwood floor. There was no wind, and there are no vents in the area.

During one of our October 2011 tours, we had a previous tenant of the building participate. She asked us if we were going to Jilly's and explained that she had rented that building for her bakery for several years. She asked if the little boy was still there. Evidently, her sons (grown men) did not like to descend into the basement because they had experienced a little boy's presence down there. She also said that they would come in early in the morning to bake and find their ovens already heated up for them, even though they had double-checked that the ovens were off when they left the night before.

Sadly, Jilly's closed its doors in December 2011.

New tenants are now moving in and have offered us the chance once again to bring our tours into the old morgue below their business.

Happy Lucky's and the Gambler's Ghost

236 Walnut Street

In 1879, Fort Collins built a firehouse, city building and jail in one short block of Walnut Street. Like so many Wild West jails built in the 1800s, the jail consisted of one aboveground cell, as well as several cells built below ground, including a solitary confinement cell made of stone. The aboveground cell, used primarily for temporary prisoners, was called a calaboose. *Calaboose* is

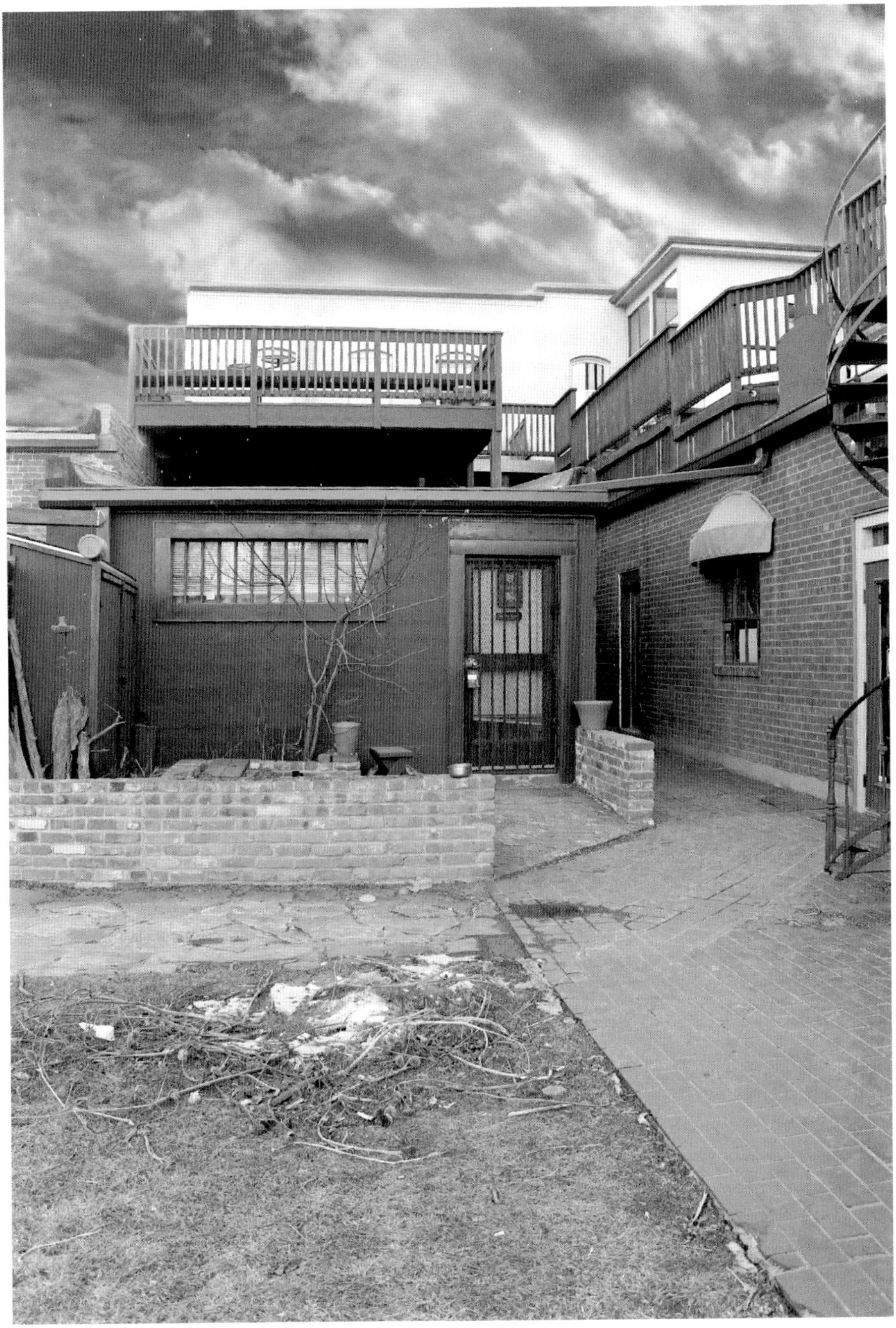

The old calaboose.

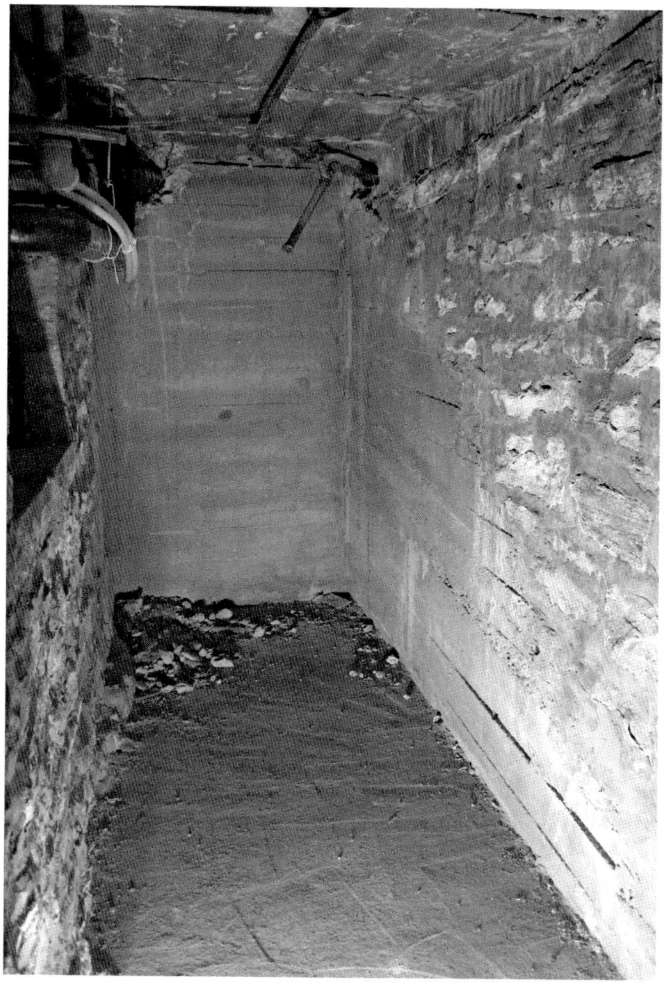

The solitary confinement cell under Happy Lucky's (old firehouse).

a Spanish word for "dungeon," and the cell lived up to the nickname. An 1880s report from the local newspaper, *Rocky Mountain News*, described the jail as one of the filthiest and most vile places on earth.

Early habitants of the jail included murderers, bank robbers and drunks. Jail keepers were known for their harsh treatment of their prisoners and the exorbitant death rate among their charges, some likely due to brutality but most from disease and pestilence.

As terrible and fearsome as the jail was, one small section struck dread in the hearts of those subject to its clammy, cold confines. The underground solitary confinement cell was only a few feet wide and about ten feet long. The stone walls were almost two feet thick, and when the heavy door slammed shut, the darkness and isolation was absolute. Prisoners of the cell lost their ability to tell the passage of time, their health and, often, their minds.

Legend has it that an Old West gambler, Jack Cassidy, ended up in the solitary confinement cell after a night of dealing dirty cards in a local saloon. Old Jack was taken into custody by a sheriff who may well have protected him from worse at the hands of those he had cheated. A man cheating at cards was fair game for gun-toting, angry men who had lost their paychecks to him, and jail was a safe haven at that point.

Upon descending the stairs to the jail and realizing that many of the inmates likely had lost money to Jack, the sheriff announced that the prisoner would spend the night in the solitary confinement cell for his own protection. Jack begged the sheriff not to throw him into solitary. He had a pathological fear of small spaces and loathed the dark. The sheriff had no patience for a man with such fears and thought a night in the cold, dark cell would teach Jack a lesson. One can only imagine Jack's horror as the heavy wooden door slammed shut and locked him into the small sandstone cell. The darkness was absolute and closed in on him like an evil cloak. Jack likely cowered on the floor, gasping for air, heart racing at the thought of being completely alone, entombed beneath the ground with no new air to breathe.

The next morning, when the sheriff went to take Jack some breakfast, he found him dead on the floor. The sheriff listed cause of death as "anxiety." There are those who say that Jack was literally "scared to death."

A male presence haunts the jail morgue next to these cells. On a recent tour, one tour patron snapped a photograph of a male face in the morgue basement. Perhaps it's Jack, still trying to find his way out to the sunlight.

Moe's BBQ: The Blackboard Apparition and Her Flying Spatulas

181 North College Avenue

Moe's BBQ is one of those places where the savory scent of home cooking draws passersby in the front door. Once inside, visitors notice that the vintage building still has a lot of the original vestiges of the Old West. Wood floors,

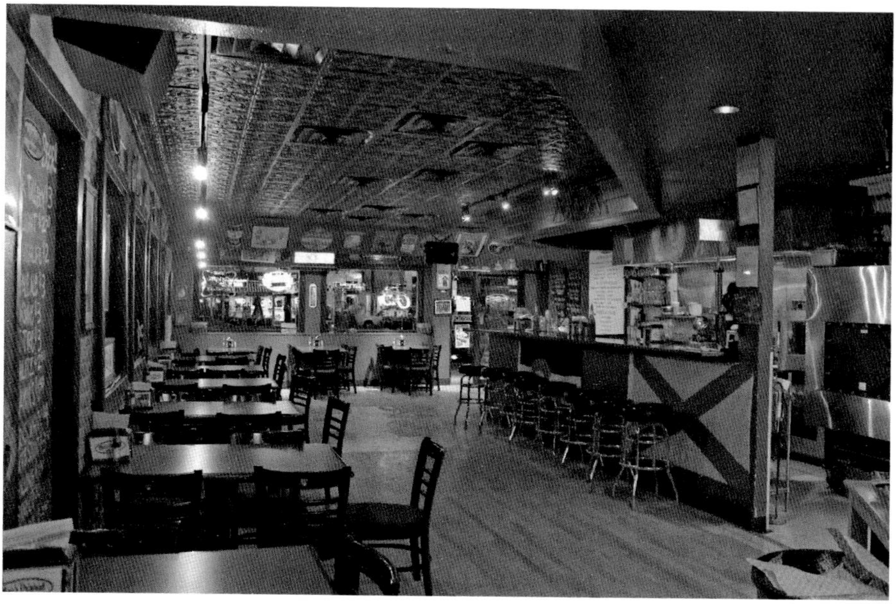

The interior of Moe's.

copper ceiling tiles and an old wood bar the length of the room make you feel like you just walked backward in history.

When Ted started this restaurant, there was a lot of remodeling to be done. He and his contractor worked night and day to prepare the building, and it wasn't long before they noticed there might be someone else there with them.

On Christmas Eve, the contractor was working in the basement. The entire building was locked up tight, and he had just come in to get a head start on work planned for the next week after Christmas. He was surprised to hear footsteps on the wood floor above him and ran up the stairs to see who had entered the locked building. No one was there. He returned to the basement, only to hear the footsteps again. Once again, he ran to the top of the stairs, only to find the entire restaurant completely empty. Unnerved, he wrapped up his tasks and went home to spend Christmas with his family.

Once the restaurant was open, employees and customers reported other ghostly activity. A spatula rose out of the crockery cup it had rested in and shot through the air and onto the ground. One employee said he went down to the basement after closing and heard a woman scream in the upstairs area of the restaurant. He ran up the stairs to see what had happened, but there was no one there.

One evening, Ted, a handful of employees and a room full of customers saw a filmy apparition come right out of the blackboard menu wall and float to the middle of the room before disappearing. Stunned, employees and customers alike circled the area trying to find an explanation for the phenomenon they had just witnessed. No reasonable conclusion could be reached. Perhaps it was the same entity that insists on throwing spatulas out of the crockery and walks the floors when no one is there. In any case, Ted and his employees keep an eye and an ear out for the spirit who haunts the barbecue joint. If you ever get a hankering for good southern barbecue and aren't afraid of ghosts, go get lunch there someday. You never know who might float by your table!

The Town Pump: The Oldest (and Tiniest) Bar in Fort Collins

124 North College Avenue

If you want to step into a real Old West saloon, stop by the Town Pump. It's tiny—it claims to be the smallest bar in Colorado, and it's probably right—but it's truly the "real deal" of Old West bars. Stop in to wet your whistle, but bring cash, as that's the only currency they take.

The Town Pump was opened in 1909 and has continually been a watering hole for the citizens of Fort Collins for over one hundred years. It is the oldest bar in town. Interestingly, it opened during the long prohibition period here in Fort Collins that lasted from 1896 to 1969. According to records, the Town Pump served 3.2 percent beer and other light refreshments during the early years, but there are multiple stories of a wild speakeasy that served hard liquor down in the Town Pump basement.

Over the years, this establishment has been known for its hauntings. There is a long shelf of liquor bottles and glasses that runs along the wall behind the bar. It isn't unusual for a glass to come flying off the shelf with absolutely no provocation or anyone near it. An employee also reports that the bathroom is haunted. She has seen the trash can rise by about a centimeter on its own with no other apparent force causing the elevation.

For many years, the basement held the feeling of a presence and gave a bit of a chill to all who entered it. One employee tells us she was nervous going down there and always felt that there was some kind of spirit in one of the lower areas. One night, just as she started up the stairs from the basement, she sensed a woman watching her from the basement. The woman was in wretched condition and looked like she had been drenched with water. Her demeanor and searching look gave the employee the impression that the woman was badly in need of help.

Disturbed by the desperate presence, the employee asked a team of intuitive ghost hunters to visit and see if they could help. According to the team, they were able to help the woman move on. The employee reports that the basement actually feels much better now, and she no longer feels that the woman is there when she goes down the stairs.

CAFÉ ARDOUR AND THE GHOST OF MADAME MARIE LAFITTE

255 Linden Street

On the first block of Linden Street heading north from Old Town Square stands two of the first buildings ever to be built in Fort Collins. On the corner of Linden and Jefferson was "Old Grout," as it was fondly called. This building was the courthouse, meeting hall and any number of things as uses and needs were identified. It is now a charming and environmentally conscious dry goods store.

Next door to this building is Café Ardour, a wonderful little coffeehouse with almost a New Orleans feel to it. Upon entering, one can almost hear the spirited conversations in French and smell the expensive perfume of the woman who built her business there over one hundred years ago—Marie LaFitte. Marie was a local businesswoman who always had one foot in legitimate business and the other foot in less legal affairs. Articulate and intelligent, she defended herself in court many times over the years, winning the respect, if not the approval, of many more upstanding local residents.

Marie was strong willed and a true survivor, born into poverty and determined to succeed. She went into the business of making sweets and set up shop down south in Pueblo. In 1902, she moved her sweet shop from Pueblo to Fort Collins, where Café Ardour is now.

A Mr. James VandeWark was the hired porter who was commissioned to move her shop and all accoutrements from Pueblo to Fort Collins. When Marie's things were delivered, she deemed that he had not done an acceptable job and refused to pay him. VandeWark took her to court, and the judge ordered Marie to pay $5,000 in damages to Mr. VandeWark.

Marie balked at paying the excessive sum of $5,000 but did pay Mr. VandeWark the original agreed-upon fee and considered the issue to be done.

Over the years, Marie was a frequent defender in the court system. In addition to selling sweets, she trafficked in bootleg liquor and ran a house of prostitution. Rumor has it that she would avoid the label of "selling alcohol" by giving away a pint of whiskey after overcharging for tobacco. Now and then, the law would call her up on charges, and she was dragged off to jail and, eventually, court.

Marie was an intelligent woman and insisted on defending herself in court rather than engaging a lawyer. Her articulate and logical arguments often got her acquitted of the crimes for which she stood trial.

She was also known for her sharp tongue and coarse language. The townspeople disdained her for this, along with her chosen professions and businesses. She was not revered in Fort Collins, but she ran a profitable business and amassed a respectable amount of money. She had purchased her own home by 1902.

George Salisbury, a local businessman, took Marie to court several times over the years regarding a property dispute. The animosity between the two was palpable and grew throughout the years. George engaged Marie in a long legal battle, little by little eroding any financial security she had managed to acquire. By 1905, he had even been granted her house on Jefferson Street by the courts.

Rather than waiting for the sheriff to evict Marie, George went to the home, forced his way in and beat Marie about the head and shoulders with his cane. He knocked out her teeth and caused her great physical harm. Marie lived the rest of her life in a pauper's hospital. A legal case against Mr. Salisbury for this egregious attack found in her favor in 1911, but she died in the hospital before she could receive the judgment.

Marie was a strong personality with a vivid presence. Even today, there are those who claim she frequents the streets of Linden and Jefferson.

Employees of Café Ardour, Marie's old sweet shop and probable brothel, report feeling a presence near the back of the store from time to time and hearing movement when there is no one there.

THE WILD BOAR AND ITS PLAYFUL SPIRITS

1510 South College Avenue

Looking for a great cup of coffee, an Old World atmosphere and some amazing and eclectic food to go along with your quest for ghosts? Stop by the Wild Boar.

The building that houses the Wild Boar was constructed in 1924 by a Mr. Bradley using beautiful rock and wood architecture. It is absolutely lovely even today and a favorite place for college students to study and families to socialize.

Mr. Bradley owned the local Cadillac dealership, and when the home was new, the entire basement was a storage area for Cadillacs. Later, the basement was finished and used for living area and storage.

The Bradley family also owned a ranch up in Estes Park, and during the winter, they closed up the ranch and brought their wranglers down the mountain to stay with them in their home. The entire attic became a dormitory for the wranglers.

Over the years, the Bradleys sold the home, and it spent time as a fraternity and then a property management office. In 2007, the owners of the Wild Boar bought the building and have run the restaurant there ever since.

Soon after they moved in, they noticed they were not alone. Susan, one of the owners, set up her office in the attic. She began to see a little girl in puffed sleeves and an apron, about eight years old, playing peekaboo around furniture and corners in the office. The little girl was such a physical presence that the first time Susan saw her she thought it was a living girl, and she wanted to know how she got there. Then the little girl disappeared into thin air, and Susan realized she had seen a ghost.

Over the years, the little girl has appeared to others as well. When the air-conditioning repairman came to check on their system, he went up to the attic and soon came to find Susan to ask if she had ever seen anything

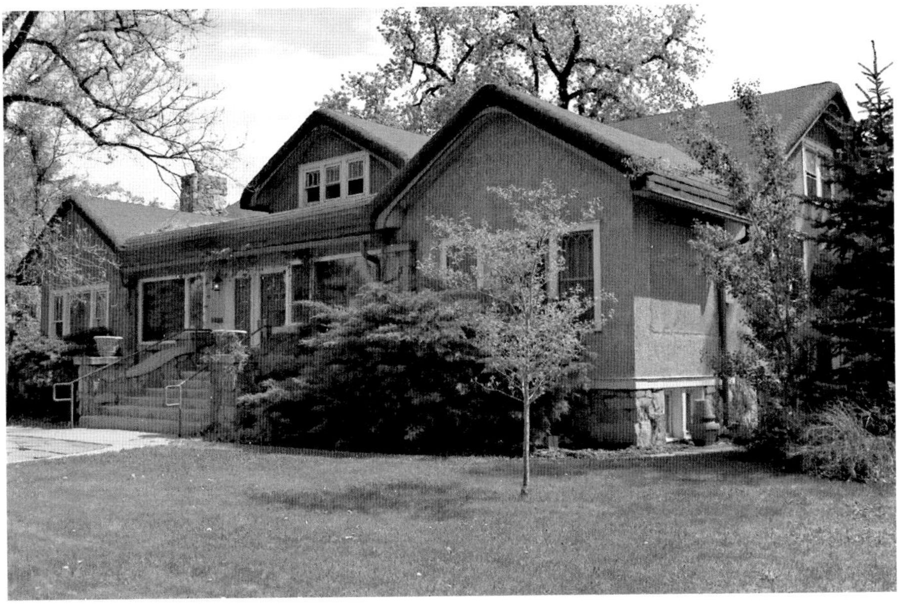

Wild Boar Coffee.

strange up there. She laughed and asked if he had seen the little girl, and it turns out he had. He said she was playing peekaboo with him, too.

The little girl ghost also likes to move things around. Objects would slide across the desk with no other physical explanation when she was around, and windows would open by themselves. The windows in the building opened by turning a knob, and at the end of the evening, the owners or employees would close the windows before going home. More than once, they would close a window only to witness the knob turning on its own and opening the window right back up.

Now and then, they would hear the little girl giggling and running around. One evening, Erik, one of the owners, went out to buy milk for the next morning and came back to the restaurant at about 11:00 p.m. As he walked in, he heard noises and then footsteps running across the floor. A little apprehensive, he quickly dropped the milk in the refrigerator and looked around the building, worried that someone had broken in. There was no living soul in the building with him, yet footsteps running through the halls could be heard.

Susan says they believe there were eight or nine ghosts residing in the building. Down in the wine cellar, a man has been seen many times. Some think it may be the ghost of Bradley himself. Once, Susan came in to open the restaurant early in the morning, went downstairs to the basement and found a woman in a long dress sitting in a chair at a table. Dismayed, Susan thought perhaps they had locked someone in at the end of the previous night's shift. As she approached the table, she noticed that the woman had her hair up in a bun, but suddenly the woman just vanished.

Among the other ghosts seen was a man in 1940s casual dress, wearing an old T-shirt. He didn't seem to notice anyone around him but walked across the room, right through a wall and out the other side of the wall. Interestingly, we were told that the wall is a fairly recent addition to the building and was not there in the time frame this man would have lived.

One of the employees, Sammy, told us that she was working behind the counter one night and felt someone blow in her ear. She thought someone had snuck up behind her to startle her and turned around. There was no one there. Dubious, she turned back to the counter, and again—this time even stronger—she felt someone blowing into her ear.

In addition to small things moving about and windows opening and closing on their own, larger, heavier items like bags of change and a heavy espresso tamper have been seen flying off counters on their own.

Susan and Erik say that the buildings around them have experienced similar hauntings and were all built by Mr. Bradley around the same time. They don't feel like any of the ghosts have ever been threatening, and Susan said she actually liked having them around.

Visiting the Wild Boar is an interesting and even comforting experience as the entire restaurant occupies this beautiful home. Stop by sometime, try the food and see if you meet anyone who might want to play a game of peekaboo with you!

Old Town Businesses

Some of Our Favorite Haunts

Frank Miller's Extraordinary Life (and Afterlife): Nature's Own Ghost

Miller Block, 11 Old Town Square and the Linden Hotel (now Nature's Own), Corner of Walnut and Linden Streets

In 1882, Danish immigrant Frank Miller came to Fort Collins from Black Hawk. By 1894, he had built the Miller Block, a beautiful building that still graces Old Town Square.

Back in the silver boom days, many of the finer buildings of Old Town were erected with fine cornices, higher-end brick from the kilns of Auntie Stone and Mr. Peterson and foundations of sandstone quarried from the town of Stout, now immersed below Horsetooth Reservoir.

Even among these quality-built blocks, the Miller Block stood out. The cost to build this solid and stately block was over $20,000—a princely sum in those days. There were those who said Mr. Miller was crazy for spending that kind of money on construction, but he said he wanted a building that would last for 500 years. The building is now over 115 years old and looks just as grand as it likely did the day it was finished.

Frank Sr., a born entrepreneur, opened the Fair Store to sell dry goods and a liquor business in the building. Two years later, in 1896, the town of

Fort Collins enforced prohibition, and Mr. Miller closed the liquor side of the endeavor.

Frank hoped his son, Frank Jr., would follow in his footsteps and left the store to him when he died. Frank Jr. had other dreams, however, and was not cut out to be tied to one place, showing up day in and day out managing a store. He longed for excitement and travel—and possibly fame. He soon sold out to a partner in the business, took the money and went on the road to find his destiny.

An excellent marksman, Frank applied to *Buffalo Bill's Wild West Show* to become a trick shooter and soon joined it in its travels. He and Buffalo Bill became good friends over the years.

After many years of travel with the *Wild West Show*, Frank came back to Larimer County to settle down. He bought the Trail's End Ranch at the end of Trail Creek and spent the staggering sum of over $100,000 making it into a guest ranch with a zoo and a Wild West show. He hosted guests over the years from all over America and over twenty-five foreign countries. Buffalo Bill was a frequent visitor, and even Will Rogers came to stay at Trail's End Ranch.

Frank loved his animals and had "tame" bears, lions and even skunks. His zoo had over 1,400 animals and became famous for being the only Wild West zoo in existence and the largest privately held zoo in America. Frank lovingly cared for his critter friends and used to take his "pet bear" in his car on errands around Fort Collins. This bear was also known for drinking beer out of a bottle. Oddly, this was not the only story of a Fort Collins resident having a bear as a pet, but that's another story.

Frank was also a talented artist and photographer. Many of his photos and paintings still grace the halls of Fort Collins establishments and have been instrumental in recording the history of the area.

Over the years, Frank's large living took its toll; his fortune turned, and his money petered away. In 1939, Frank lost his ranch and, soon after, his wife. In 1946, his son was killed. We're told that he spent his last years in relative poverty. He went to live at the Linden Hotel and, in exchange for his room, provided it with his artwork to sell in the lobby.

Frank passed away of a heart attack in 1953 at the ripe old age of eighty-seven. He had led an adventurous and interesting life, fulfilling the dreams of his youth.

His ghost is sometimes seen in the lobby of the old Linden Hotel (now Nature's Own) underneath one of his paintings that now hangs in the back corner of the store. He stands there, looking out on what was once his final home. When someone approaches to speak with him, he slowly fades away. His roots here are strong, and it's no surprise that he still looks in on his beloved hometown.

The Welch Block Fire of 1880 and a Poltergeist in the Present-Day Building

100 West Mountain Street

It was a cold February night in 1880, and James Howe was walking down the sidewalk in the middle of town about 11:00 p.m. This is the same James Howe mentioned in our previous story of murder and lynching, and it seems he may have been working his way home this particular evening from yet another night of drinking. He smelled smoke faintly as he walked south, and as he neared the Welch Block, he saw flames dancing in the windows of the building. He ran to alert the volunteer fire department, and within minutes, a brigade of men toiled to rescue occupants and put out the flames that had by that time fully engulfed the building.

The Welch Block is now the building that houses Austin's Restaurant on the corner of College Avenue and Mountain Street. In 1880, it was the site of a dry goods store, law office, assorted other businesses and small apartments in the upstairs areas. At the time of the fire, twelve people lived in the building, and there were two employees of various establishments still on site as well.

Upon smelling smoke and feeling the increasing heat of the flames, upstairs residents began to stir, and realizing fire had broken out in their building, they frantically searched for safety. Mrs. Welch jumped from the second story with her grandchildren. Though injured by the twelve-foot fall, they all survived.

Miss Tilly Irving, only twenty years old, woke to the sound of her screaming neighbors and glanced out her window to discover smoke and flames. Neighbors pounded on her door and implored her to leave immediately. Being a modest young woman, she declined to open the door and refused to leave until she had a chance to put her petticoat on. No decent woman would be seen out on the street without her petticoat, and fire was no excuse for such a breach of the moral code! Alas, she took too long to ready herself for escape and succumbed to the flames. Her charred remains were found on the floor below her room.

When light of morning dawned and the fire had been doused, another fatality was found. A.F. Hopkins, age twenty-four and clerk of one of the businesses, was found in a back closet of the building. The rescue crew was shocked to discover that the clerk had died, not from the fire, but from a bullet wound! Someone had shot him and hid him in the closet, they surmised, and then lit the fire to cover the crime. Perhaps he had walked in and interrupted a burglary?

This building has experienced continual spiritual "disruptions" but none so vivid as the more recent accounts of poltergeist activity in the business this building now houses.

Poltergeists are mischievous spirits. They tend to attach to a person or a beloved item, and they usually only stay around for a short time. While they hang around, however, they wreak havoc on the physical surroundings and the mental state of the poor soul to whom they're attached.

One such poltergeist manifested in 2003, when the Dandelion/Clothes Pony store moved into the old Welch Block building and began to renovate the space. We talked to Dave, the husband of one of the owners, about his experiences during this time, which we had originally read about in Nancy Hansford's book *Northern Colorado Ghost Stories*.

Dave told us that he was in the process of painting the interior of the store at about four o'clock in the morning. He had just grabbed a bucket of blue paint and climbed the ladder, setting the bucket on the top platform of the ladder. All of a sudden, he smelled the strong scent of rain, although it was not raining outside. At the same time, he saw an oily film forming in front of him that to this day he really doesn't know how to describe. The paint bucket then shot sideways a few feet, falling to the ground but not tipping and spilling as would normally happen.

Later that morning, another owner came in and stepped into the ladies' room. She locked the door and then, feeling a bit uneasy for no apparent reason, went to unlock it again. The door would not unlock, and she found herself trapped. She cried for help, and Dave tried to unlock it from the outside with a key. It remained locked. Ultimately, they ended up knocking down the door to get her out. They had experienced no trouble with the lock prior to that morning.

According to owners and employees of the store, the activity stopped as suddenly as it had started once the remodel job was over. They've had no experiences since and feel the store is "clean" of any spirits.

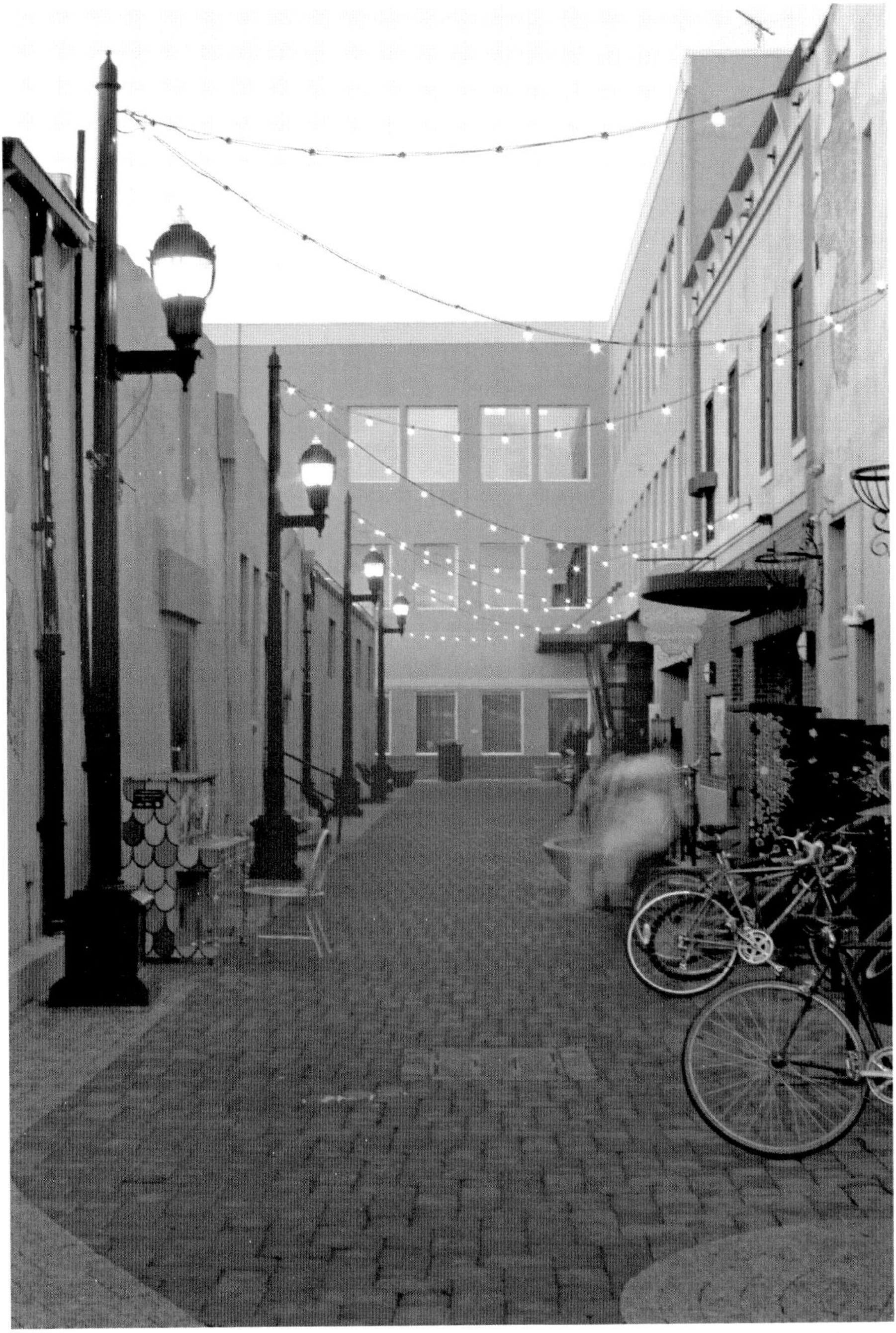

A possible apparition in the alley behind the Clothes Pony.

On one of our tours this past summer, we stopped in the back alley behind the store to tell the story, and a man on the tour raised his hand. He asked if we were going into the basement of the store. When we replied we weren't, he expressed relief. He had worked for the phone company and been summoned to install phone lines in that basement during the summer of 2003. He reported the extraordinarily strong feeling of being watched for two days down in that basement while he worked, although there was no one else down there. In one area of the basement, the air was significantly colder for no apparent reason. He told us he felt there was someone right there where the cold spot was, watching his every move. He was extremely glad when his work was done and told us he'd never go back in that basement again.

Recently, one of Fort Collins Tours owners, Chris, was taking pictures of the Old Town area for fun and with the idea of including some of them in this book. It was mid-afternoon on a sunny day, and he wasn't expecting any anomalous activity in the pictures. He set up his tripod in the alley behind the Dandelion/Clothes Pony and took several pictures. In one picture, he captured what looks like a headless, chubby figure sitting on one of the planters at the back entrance to the store. After searching for every physical, photographic and scientific explanation, we can say only that we don't know what this is, but it looks like a possible apparition. Could it be Miss Tilly Irving, the young woman who perished in the fire, enjoying a sunny day in the alley behind the building?

THE GHOST OF TRIMBLE COURT

In 1880–81, Ed Trimble and business associates built the Opera Galleria in hopes of lending a more cultured and entertaining hue to Fort Collins. The stage at the Opera Galleria featured musical acts and plays and hosted political rallies and community meetings.

Ed Trimble was involved in the daily business of the Galleria for many, many years. He used to stay until closing and then would walk, using his silver cane, out the front door of the Opera Galleria, across College Avenue and through the alley now known as Trimble Court.

Ed also owned his own billiard parlor at 132 North College Avenue and was written up in a 1905 Chamber of Commerce brochure as being

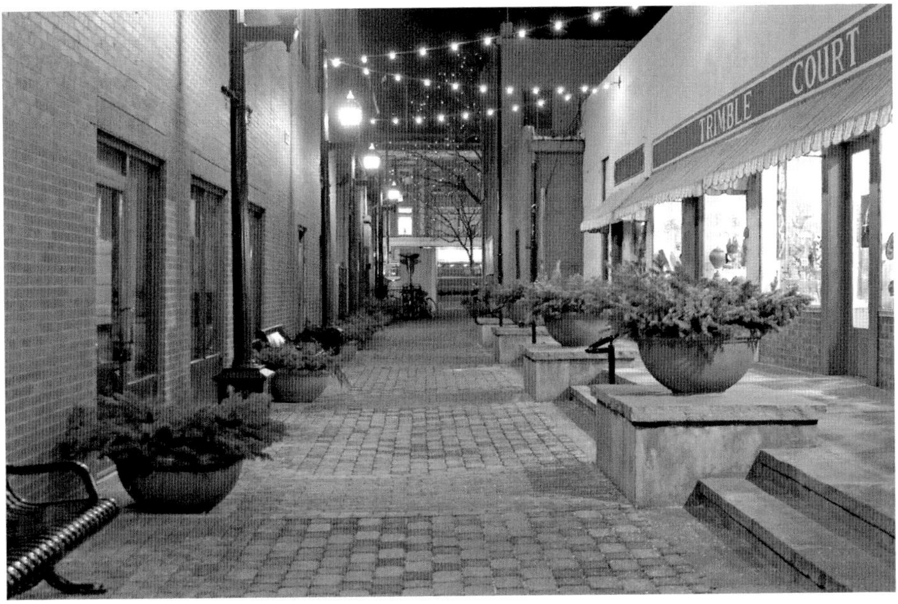

Trimble Court.

"a man of pleasing address, candid, and intelligent, and well qualified to bring to success any enterprise in which he might embark. He takes a deep interest in the affairs of the city and, like many other of our wide-awake citizens, is strongly in favor of agitating for another railroad to and from the city."

Ed reportedly worked up until the day he died, the silver cane ever at his side. He was a man of habit, and it isn't surprising to hear that after all of those decades working and living in the area of Trimble Court, old Ed frequently manifested as an apparition there. People strolling through the alley report seeing a man in an old-time black suit playing a fiddle or a violin while standing with his back to the south wall of Trimble Court. As they approach him to see what he is playing, he disappears.

Others have spoken of seeing a man's apparition traversing the Opera Galleria itself and hearing accompanying footsteps. Ed's magnificent work ethic seems to have followed him beyond the grave—even now, he seems determined to show up for work.

THE OLD TOWN ART AND FRAMERY AND THE BOOTLEGGER'S GHOST

173 North College Avenue

Early Fort Collins had a little war going on: the war between those who shunned alcohol and those who imbibed.

In 1883, the town of Fort Collins survey listed fewer than one thousand residents, with five brothels serving liquor and thirteen bars. The more conservative settlers and founding families felt that the preponderance of alcohol had become the root of crime in their town and an attractant for a rougher crowd. In fact, the very industries that settled the town brought with them a kind of social "collateral damage." Silver miners, agricultural workers and cowhands all flocked to the area for work, bringing with them a thirst for alcohol and recreation. They spent their evenings in the town brothels, bars and numerous gambling establishments. Not surprisingly, most of the local sheriff's resources were expended sorting out brawls and other crimes after dark at these local gatherings.

Temperance leagues, mostly staffed by the town women, were formed to begin a movement toward banning alcohol in Fort Collins. There was an early attempt at prohibition, but the bars found the fines for providing alcohol more affordable than the liquor licenses had been when selling drinks was legal. Therefore, prohibition did little to slow down the alcohol sales and consumption in this wild Old West town. Finally, in 1896, the temperance leagues won the war, and alcohol became illegal in Fort Collins. The prohibition lasted for seventy-four years and was not lifted until 1969.

In the middle of this war stood the businesses involved in the brewing and bottling of alcohol. Fort Collins Bottling Works bottled alcohol, beer and soda pop throughout the late 1800s and into the early 1900s. When prohibition finally became law, Robert Miller, the proprietor of the bottling works, declared that he would bottle only soda pop and 3.2 percent beer, which was still allowed under the statutes.

As time went on, the local police began to notice that alcohol was still flowing in the areas surrounding the bottle works. They also heard rumors of tunnels that led from the bottle works to the nearby hotels and brothels, but they couldn't find any hard evidence that they existed. From time to time over the next few years, the sheriff would send over some men to talk to

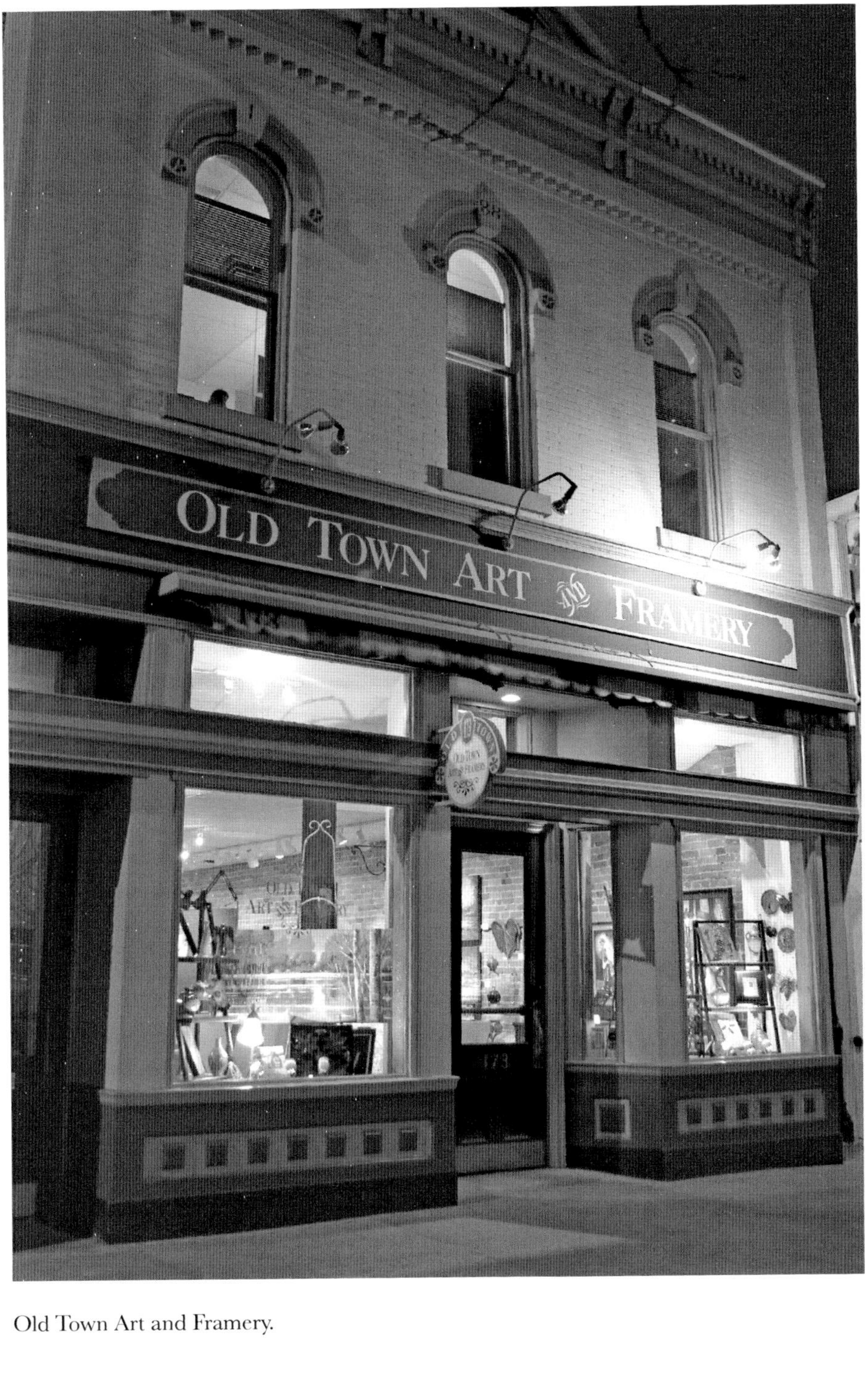

Old Town Art and Framery.

Robert Miller, and Miller always denied that Fort Collins Bottle Works was in the business of bootlegging. It was a tough call for the local sheriff, not only because this case of bootlegging was hard to prove, but also because Robert Miller was a well-loved and highly respected member of the Fort Collins community.

Finally, in 1905, nine years after prohibition had been instituted, the sheriff sent a raid into the Fort Collins Bottle Works. Police entered through the front door and confronted Robert Miller's son, asking to speak to Robert. Robert came up from the back, walked around to the front of the bar and stated to the waiting police that they were not welcome to search his establishment. The lead police captain responded that Miller had no choice. They had a warrant; he was under suspicion of bottling hard liquor, and they fully intended to find it. He directed his men to commence the search.

Robert Miller became enraged and demanded that they cease their search of his building immediately. When he realized he was going to be ignored, he picked up a full beer bottle and flung it viciously at the head of a nearby lawman. The beer bottle cracked against the man's head, exploding with shards of glass and foaming beer. The lawman, stunned by the attack, instinctively turned, drew his gun and fired in the direction of Miller. The shot hit Miller squarely in the heart. He stumbled backward, fell over the bar and died within minutes.

Stunned, the entire town grieved the passing of Robert Miller. He had been a local businessman since the town was just a settlement and was loved by many. The lawman pleaded self-defense and was acquitted of any wrongdoing. Still, the guilt and stigma of his actions haunted him, and he was shunned by many in the small town for killing Miller.

Over the years, Robert Miller's ghost has often been seen walking down the back stairs of the old bottling works, now the home of Old Town Art and Framery. He likely walked down those stairs most days of his life for over forty years, and perhaps his spirit just wasn't ready to leave the business and town he loved so much. Disembodied footsteps are also heard on the hardwood floor inside the building from time to time, leaving one to wonder if Robert Miller still goes about his daily business there.

Marcy Oliver and her family now own the building and Old Town Art and Framery. Marcy shared with us that a few years ago the grandson of the lawman who shot Robert Miller came by and gave her a newspaper article and other information that he had written concerning the incident from his grandfather's point of view. His grandfather had greatly grieved killing

Miller and had never truly gotten over it. Never before or after this incident had he discharged his weapon while on duty.

As we tell this story on the tours and visit the gallery, we sometimes wonder if the footsteps on the hardwood floor may in fact belong to the lawman rather than Robert Miller. Perhaps he has returned to apologize and make peace for a split-second reaction he regretted the rest of his life.

Happy Jack and His Long Stay at Old Grout

261 Linden (now Green-Logic)

The legends of Happy Jack, a notorious criminal of the Old West, continue to puzzle. It seems that the moniker "Happy Jack" may have been assigned to more than one criminal, and therefore the abundance of crimes may not be attributed to just one man.

That being said, we have one Happy Jack who frequented Larimer County and seems to have remained in spirit at one of the oldest sites of the Fort Collins original settlement.

The sheriff at the time was Joe Mason. Joe was the first settler in Fort Collins, having originally moved from Canada to LaPorte. He was instrumental in helping the military relocate its post from LaPorte to present-day Old Town following the flood of 1864 that washed the entire camp downstream.

Mason opened the first sutler's (general) store, fondly dubbed "Old Grout" by the townspeople. Old Grout became central to the town and was used as the post office, court, community hall and jail at various times.

Happy Jack was, among other things, a horse thief. There were few more reviled creatures in the Old West than men who would steal another man's horse. He led a band of outlaws marauding through northern Colorado stealing horses and livestock from less protected homesteads and ranches.

In the early 1870s, Happy Jack and his gang were caught rustling livestock in the Fort Collins area. Joe Mason, now sheriff, arrested the men and tossed them into the upper floor at Old Grout to contain them. It wasn't long before the makeshift jail was visited and the outlaws hauled out for a "necktie party." One by one, each prisoner was hanged by a noose thrown over a tree limb. They would dangle for a while and then be let back down. The object

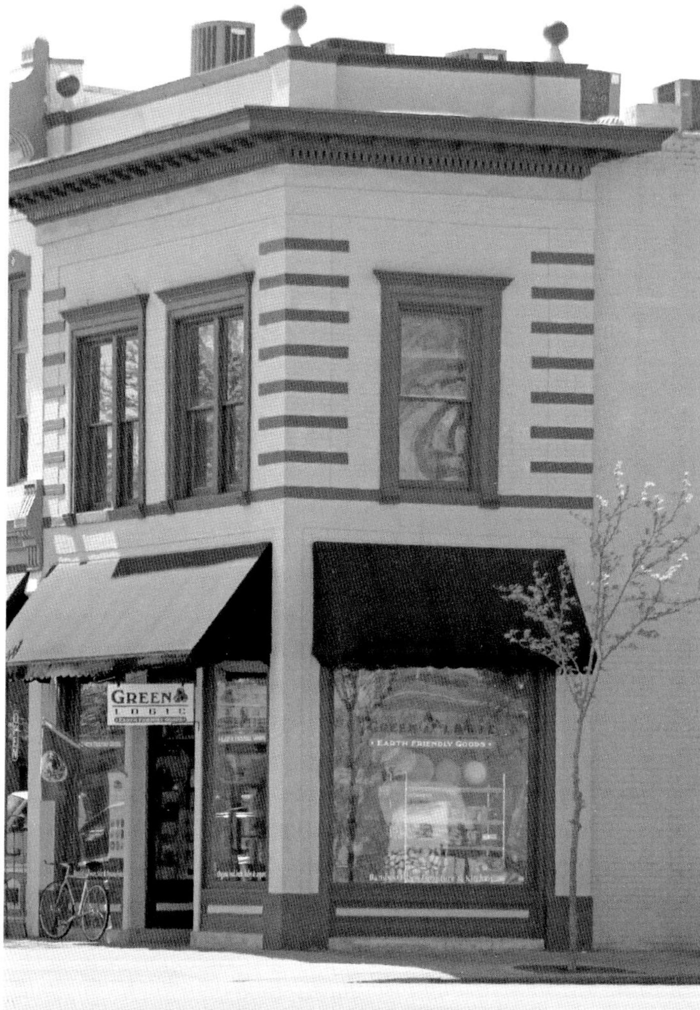

Old Grout.

was to scare them, not kill them, and it seems that was accomplished. Special attention was paid to Happy Jack, the ringleader, who was left to dangle for especially long and uncomfortable periods of time.

Once released, the gang was admonished never to come back, and according to one account, it never did.

Another story, though, indicated that Happy Jack stuck around or returned to the area later. Again caught thieving horses, he had landed in jail but managed to escape. He made his way to a local ranch, where he found the rancher's wife alone and unprotected. He committed what they called in Victorian times an "abomination" against the woman, and once again Sheriff Mason was called. Mason tied Happy Jack to a post, handed the wronged woman a gun and implored her to just shoot him. She didn't have the stomach for it, though, so Mason hauled Jack back to jail.

Sometime during the night, legend has it that Happy Jack once again escaped. The townspeople were all livid at his apparent freedom, except for, strangely enough, the wronged woman's male relatives. Happy Jack was never seen again.

Years later, when the original Old Grout building was taken down to build a newer building, rumor has it that one of the woman's brothers stopped by to check on the progress of the demolition. One of the workers turned to the brother and asked if he would find the body of Happy Jack in the walls of the old building. The brother just shrugged and walked away. Later that day, as they tore down the building piece by piece, they found the last clothes Happy Jack had been seen in stuffed inside a space between the inside wall and the exterior of the building. The clothes were covered in blood.

If you visit the Old Grout today, you'll find a dry goods store of modern times: Green-Logic. This lovely store is dedicated to bringing sustainable goods that promote harmony with the environment to present day residents of Fort Collins.

This store has some quirks, though. There is a stairway inside the store that goes nowhere—just up to a landing and the back wall. And in the loft above the store, there is an area where some have sensed a presence. Strange noises emanate from that area as well, and often those on the main floor can hear what sounds like things falling off shelves up in the loft.

While the presence does not seem threatening, we still wonder if it could be Happy Jack. After all, he was never found. Maybe he is still there somewhere.

Vortex Alley

Behind Curiosities and in Front of the Forge Publick House

We first heard stories of the strange and mystical qualities of the alley by the Forge Publick House in a great book by Nancy Hansford, *Northern Colorado*

Ghost Stories She wrote about an intuitive named Kim Pentecost and her exploration of that area, finding groups of spectral musicians playing in the alley and even a report of the ghost of John Entwistle from The Who hanging about back there.

Kim said there was a portal in that alley that allowed spirits to move in and out of our world from the spirit world at will. The curious thing was that all such spiritual portals are known to be above a body of water, and no body of water seemed to flow below this area.

Years later, as we took tours through the alley, we told this story regularly, although we weren't sure about the portal. Yet there was always a strange feeling in the area that Kim had pointed out, and it was undeniably somehow "different."

Kim lives in South Carolina now, and I called her to ask about her stories of Fort Collins hauntings. I have to admit that I can be a bit of a skeptic when it comes to intuitives, but I soon found her to be the "real deal" by my standard. Not two minutes into the conversation, she suddenly said to me, "You're telling a story about slaves perishing, but you're in the wrong place… It wasn't at the old train depot freight area, it was over off Mulberry." I had only told the story twice, and she would have had no way of knowing that I told it at all, let alone that I was in the train depot freight area, which is now a local restaurant. I had not mentioned that story or any others at that point.

Kim went on to say that Fort Collins is one of the most spiritually active places she has ever been. She felt a great deal of activity in the alley and believed it was a portal. She also talked about "clearing" the spirits from the area by helping them go toward the light. We've heard this before, and many businesses surrounding this alley have had mediums come in to "clear" their business of ghosts because of excessive spectral activity. The only problem in this local area seems to be that the ghosts keep coming back, which somewhat reflects the theory that a portal is a "revolving door" for spirits.

In the summer of 2011, when the Forge Publick House was getting ready to open and the guys who own it, Nathan and Avery, were there round the clock renovating the place, we stopped by to see their progress. They had pulled up an area outside to redo some of the outdoor features, and beneath the floor they had found another sub floor. Beneath that, they had found access to not only a tunnel but also the waterway that flows beneath Old Town Fort Collins! This was the missing link of the theory that a portal could be part of the spiritual activity in the area.

We've continually had tour participants snap digital photos of the area, capturing strange lights and orbs that have specific patterns above an old iron spiral staircase near the alley. The businesses surrounding this area seem to have spirits that remain or return despite many clearings, and in fact, an exorcism was performed in the Linden Hotel in the 1970s. Could it be that even if they're sent back to wherever they are supposed to go, they have the power and the will to return to their beloved Old Town?

The alley we speak of is surrounded by the back of Curiosities on Walnut, the back of the Linden (now Nature's Own) and in front of the Forge Publick House, a new and wonderful watering hole that serves a variety of beers not found elsewhere in Fort Collins. Stop by sometime and see if you see or feel anything strange or interesting. We usually do!

Déj Vu and Our Local Firehouse

If you are one day strolling down Walnut Street between College Avenue and Linden Street and suddenly feel a strange sense of déjà vu, it isn't your mind playing tricks on you. You may have actually seen these historic buildings elsewhere!

Harper Goff was a Fort Collins native whose family owned one of the local newspapers. In 1951, Harper took a trip to merry old England, and while he was there, he stopped in to a model train shop in London to take a look around. As he browsed, he came across one of the model villages with the train winding in and out of tunnels, past miniature towns and through meticulously sculpted tiny Alpine mountain passes. He was mesmerized. Harper was a visionary, and he had no remorse for letting his imagination run away with him. As he marveled at the small scene before him, another shopper stopped to admire it as well.

It wasn't long before he and the man across the train table from him struck up a conversation. The man was originally from Missouri but was now working in Southern California to develop not just a theme park but also a place that would be magical and inspiring for children and adults alike. His name was Walt Disney.

Disney was already well known for his innovation in animation by the time he started to develop the idea for Disneyland. Harper Goff had admired his work and was eager to discuss the upcoming park with him. They had a long and enjoyable conversation in the train shop, and when they parted, Walt told Harper to look him up when they were both back in the United States.

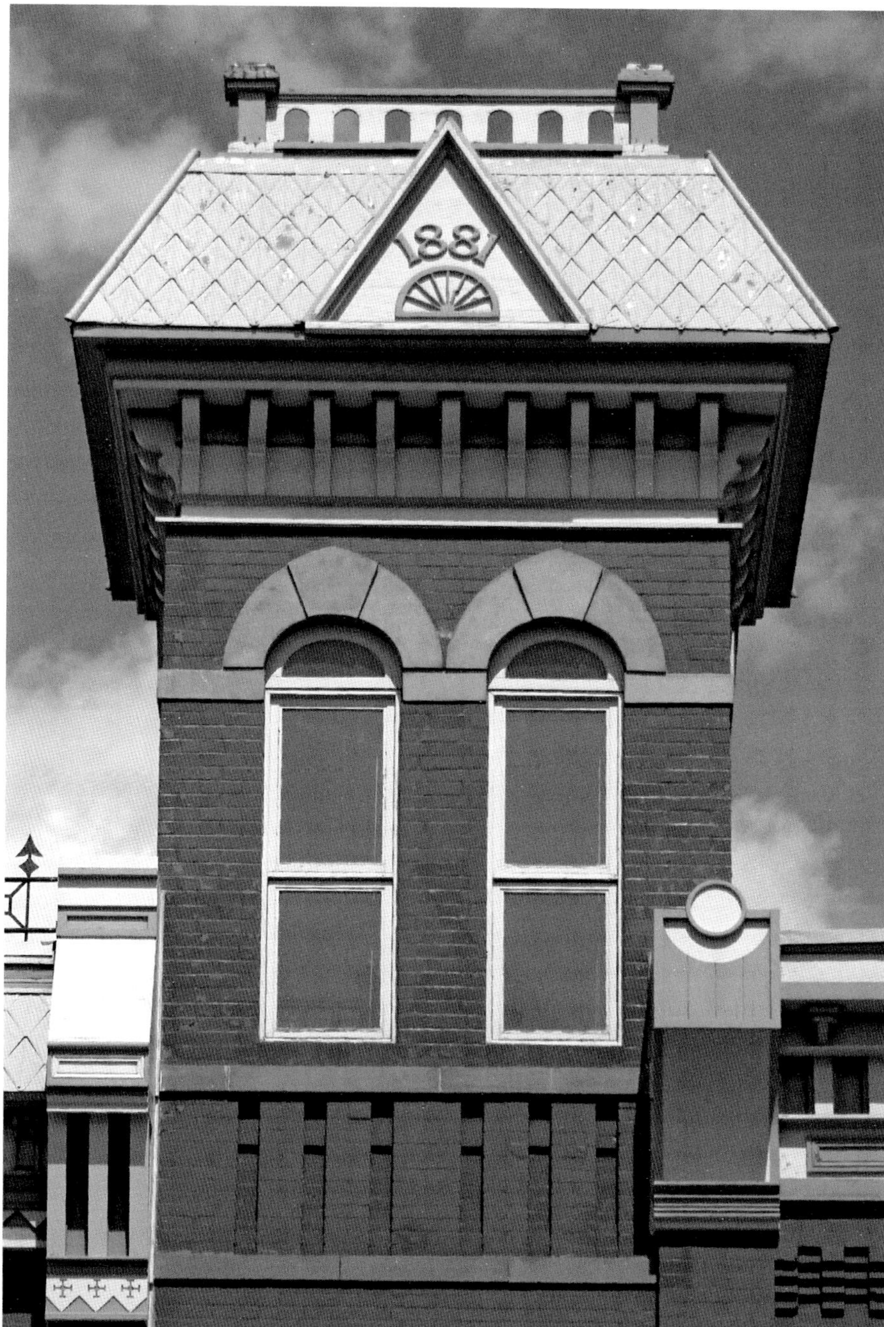

The old firehouse bell tower.

Harper did just that and eventually went to work with Disney to help develop ideas for the planned Disneyland.

One day, Harper's family mailed him some pictures of themselves. They were still in Fort Collins and no doubt missed him. Harper was thrilled to receive the pictures and wandered over to Walt's office to show him his family. Walt took one look at his pictures, complimented the family and then asked, "Where is this building?"

Harper told him it was the firehouse in his hometown, Fort Collins, Colorado. Walt had been modeling Disneyland's Main Street USA after his own hometown in Missouri, but upon seeing the firehouse, he thought he should take a trip to Fort Collins to take a look. Upon visiting, he changed his design and set his crew on the task of mimicking buildings here in Fort Collins.

If you take a trip to Disneyland in Anaheim, California, and walk in the entrance of the park onto Main Street USA, look to the left. One of the first buildings you will see is a replica of the firehouse on Walnut Street. Inside you can rent a locker to store your things, visit the first aid station and experience the hospitality of the Disneyland crew. Walk up and down Main Street USA and you may see other components of our buildings, from the ornate cornices to the old-fashioned window frames.

The firehouse in Fort Collins was built in 1881 and served as the local fire station until 1973. It is now the Firehouse Book Store, a lovely and comfortable shop dedicated to providing a quality mix of fiction and nonfiction to locals and tourists. Next door, in Happy Lucky's Teahouse, one can see the original fire pole streaming down from a second story (now an apartment) and the painted lines on the floor directing where the fire trucks should plant their wheels as they entered the station.

The bell tower of the firehouse was in past years kept sealed. There was a rope that came down through a small access door that could be pulled to ring the bell and summon the firefighters but never a door that would allow a person access to the bell tower.

Over the years, people standing across from the firehouse have reported seeing a figure up in the bell tower. Most just thought it was a night watchman or one of the firemen. However, those who know the building well and realize that there was no way to access the tower feel that the presence in the bell tower may be the ghost of one of the firefighters, just watching over the city and keeping it safe.

Local Ghosts Around Town and in Rural Areas

Suicide by Dual Gunshot Wounds in Library Park

225 Matthews Street

Alma Gault was thirty-two years of age and still unmarried. In 1909, some would say she was an old maid. Others may have admired her and thought of her as solidly independent.

Alma resided with her sister at 225 Matthews Street near Old Town. One day, a handsome man asked Alma out on a date, and she eagerly accepted. She and Mr. Edward A. Shank began "stepping out" together on a regular basis.

Her family had reservations about the budding relationship. This Mr. Shank was not someone of whom they approved. When he came to pick her up, they worried until she returned. He was not a "safe" choice of man to whom they would entrust their beloved Alma were they given the choice. Despite Alma's family's objections, before long Mr. Shank had become her fiancé.

On the cold and snowy night of January 3, 1910, Mr. Shank came and picked up Alma for a date. According to his recollection, he dropped her off safely at her home before 11:00 p.m. However, her sister became alarmed

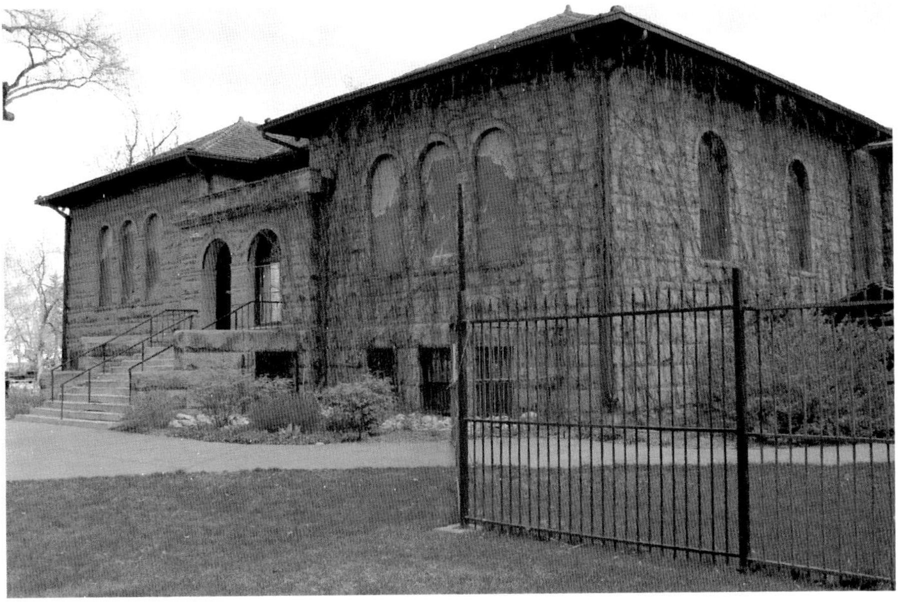

The old Carnegie Library.

when Alma had not returned by midnight, and she alerted the police. There were eyewitnesses who claimed they had seen the couple near the park arguing late in the night.

A search party was launched, and the police, family and volunteers covered the area surrounding her home in the chillingly cold early hours of the morning of January 11. As dawn broke, Alma's body was found in a snowdrift in the park adjacent to her home. She had two bullet wounds through her chest.

The coroner examined her, and an inquest was completed. Oddly enough, the death was ruled a suicide. How, we wonder, does someone shoot herself through the chest twice? It seems the first shot would disable someone to the point she'd be unable to fire again. Was there a coverup? Did Mr. Shank have some undue influence over the outcome of the investigation, or was shoddy police work at hand? These are questions that will likely go unanswered for eternity.

Perhaps Alma is still trying to answer those questions, as she and Mr. Shank are the only ones who really knew what happened that cold and fateful night. It seems the Carnegie Library adjacent to this park (the local museum up until the last few months) has been the site of some unexplained activity. Employees of the museum report that they often heard movement in the museum when no one was about, and they also experienced some weird troubles with technology. Now that the museum is empty, we wonder if Alma walks the halls in peace or if she still hopes to shed light on the circumstances of her death.

The Frat House Haunting

One night, our tour was populated almost entirely by a local fraternity. Sigma Phi Epsilon is a historic fraternity with deep roots in Fort Collins. We were surprised and delighted that evening to find that some of the businesses we visit on our tours are owned by SigEp alumni.

As we made our way around Old Town, we found that several of the sites were more active than usual. The guys from SigEp asked lots of great questions, and while they were interested in the paranormal phenomena at hand, they were equally interested in finding the "physics" behind it, if any. As we played the voice recording of a previous night's EVP with a man's voice, the electromagnetic field meter spiked. One of the young men, an engineering student, pointed out that perhaps the electricity emanating from the digital recorder had caused the spike. We assured him that we had tested that theory and that the recorder did not have the "juice" to make the EMF meter spike that strongly, if at all. He seemed a little dubious about that, so we turned off the recorder. As soon as we turned it off, the EMF began to flash furiously and beeped at the highest frequency. It seemed the ghost might be letting us know that he had listened to the conversation, so we decided to experiment. We turned the digital recorder back on, and the flashing ceased abruptly. Again, we turned it off, and the EMF meter immediately spiked at the top. We proceeded to do this several times, all with the same results.

Fascinated by this activity, which felt like communication, the young men began to tell me about the ghostly happenings in their house. They told story after story of a ghost they fondly referred to as "Fizzy," and clearly they felt he was a positive force and not something to fear. They asked if we would like to visit and take a tour of their home, and we made arrangements to go out the next week.

SigEp occupies one of the most stately homes on the Colorado State University campus. The house was built in 1929, and Sigma Phi Epsilon

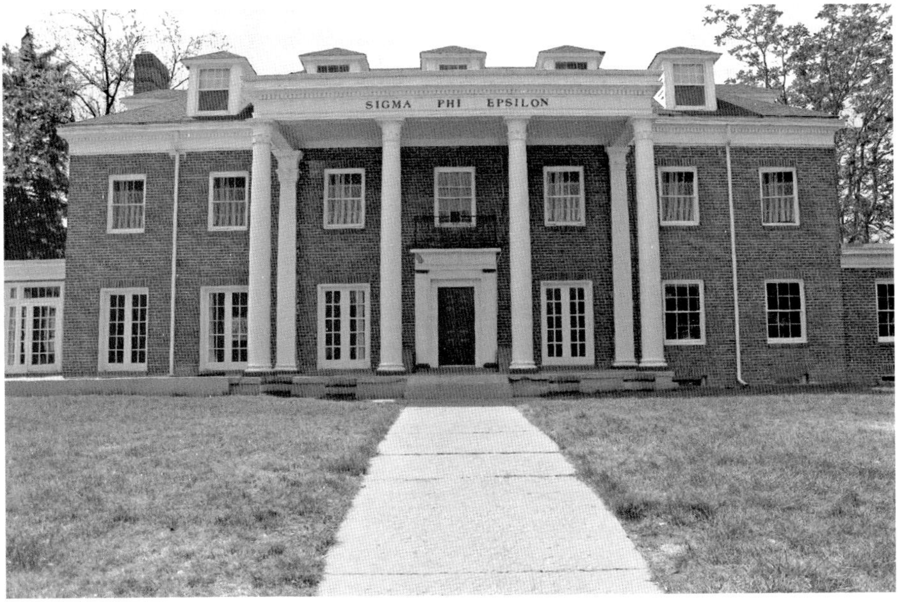

Sigma Phi Epsilon House.

moved in in 1935. There have been over 2,500 men initiated into the fraternity in the Fort Collins chapter. With pillars adorning the front and three stories of truly elegant architecture, it is reminiscent of the old antebellum mansions of the South. The interior seems even larger than the home appears from the front and houses dozens of members.

Upon arriving at the home, I was greeted by about a dozen of the guys, led by Luke, the student who had made the arrangements. We sat in a side room, and they began to share their stories.

A common story was one of hearing footsteps sprinting up and down the hallways of the second and third floors. Several residents reported being awakened between 2:00 and 4:00 a.m., thinking that some of the other guys were running around the house. The awakened person would check in the hall to see who was running around, only to find no one there accompanying the sprinting footsteps.

Another pair of residents who share a room reported that one night they had gone to bed and were just falling asleep when one of the printers in the room started to print for no reason. Startled, and thinking about Fizzy, one of the guys jumped up and yanked the power cord out of the wall to stop the printer. They settled back in and decided that maybe it was just a fluke.

Five minutes later, the alarm clock went off, and the music from the alarm continued to crescendo to blaringly loud before one of them could get to it. The alarm had not been set for that night and usually went off at the same time every morning.

In that same room, one of the guys walked in during the late evening, and a ghostly figure appeared outside his second-story window, backlit by the streetlight. The figure crossed by the window, again backlit by the streetlight, at least three times.

Other members experienced strange dreams of another student coming to them and saying, "I'm Fizzy," and then waking to find extreme pressure on their chest holding them down.

In two incidents, it seems Fizzy wanted to prevent the guys from doing something unwise. One of the guys was talking about going out on the third-story balcony to hang out (and it should be noted that the balcony has no railings to prevent falling off). The railings were removed, and the roof was sealed a few years ago due to excessive water damage. Although it was a popular hangout at one time, the gentlemen are no longer supposed to go out on the balcony for safety reasons. As soon as the suggestion was made that they go out on this unsafe balcony, all of the lights on the floor went out. When the guys went to see if a breaker had tripped, it hadn't, and as soon as they said, "Well, maybe we won't go out there," the lights went back on.

One night, a group of residents went up to the attic to hang out. The attic has some chairs and a three-pronged freestanding halogen light. There isn't enough room to stand up in the attic room, but the guys find it a comfortable place to relax and talk. One of the guys started talking about daredevil stunts, and the freestanding light fixture flew down like it had been pushed, even though no one was anywhere near it. The attic plunged into complete darkness, and the guys had to find their way to the ladder. It seems Fizzy is watching out for them.

During the summer, the third floor is closed off, and the fire door leading there is locked. One summer, there were frequently loud and clear sounds of footsteps, laughing, talking and music coming from the third floor. It sounded like there was a party going on up there. There is no exterior entrance or access to the third floor. When the maintenance crew was summoned to go up there and check on the third floor, all the doors to the bedrooms that had been closed were wide open, and the hall was full of personal effects that had been in the rooms. There had been no way for anyone to access that floor in the previous weeks since it had been locked up tight.

The third floor continues to have disturbing activity. One night, one of the guys who sleeps on the second floor heard at least two guys running up and down the hallway above at about two thirty in the morning. After a while, he decided that if his buddies upstairs were having fun, he either wanted to join them or convince them to calm down so he could get some sleep. He wandered up the stairs to the third floor, and there was no one in the hallway. Thinking they had gone into one of the rooms, he headed west down the hall and checked each room, finding all of his friends sound asleep. As he reached the very west end of the hall, he heard footsteps running down the hall toward the bathroom, which is at the east end of the hall. He turned around just in time to see the bathroom door slam shut.

"Got 'em!" he thought. He ran down the hall and knocked on the door. No one answered, so he opened the door. There was no one in the bathroom.

Not long after, another resident heard the same footsteps running up and down the hall and looked out the door of his room to see what was going on. Just as he looked toward the bathroom at the east end of the hall, the door swung open, and the shower curtain billowed out into the hall. He ran down to see who was in the bathroom, but again, there was no one there.

One night, the guys all gathered in the main room to watch *Paranormal Activity III*. After the movie, they were still hanging out watching TV, and the cable box went out. Joking about poltergeists, they tried to fix the cable box, but to no avail, so they turned off the TV. Five minutes later, the carbon monoxide detector went off loudly, and the digital display read, "Test mode." They managed to turn that off and were just getting ready for bed when the TV went back on all by itself. They believe Fizzy was having fun with them since they were already a little edgy after watching *Paranormal Activity III*.

When asked if all this activity bothered them, the guys told us that they like Fizzy and that they don't want him to go away. He's part of their home, and they look forward to hearing from him from time to time.

Ghost Dancers of the 1800s

"Are we there yet, Mommy?" came the plaintive little voice from the backseat.

"No Mackie, we're still near Fort Collins. It takes a while to get to Laramie. You just take a nap, OK?" came the reply.

Mackie was four, and his sister, Natalie, age seven, was in the backseat next to him. Mom drove, and Dad was snoozing against the passenger side window. They were headed north on the back road out of Fort Collins to visit family for the weekend.

Around dusk, the little ones in the backseat fell quiet, and Heather, their mom, thought they were napping. Instead, they were intently watching out the window. Natalie had seen deer out there before, and she told Mackie to watch for them, too.

About twenty minutes north of Fort Collins, Mackie asked, "Why are all those people by the road?"

Heather glanced from side to side, seeing nothing. "What people, Mackie?"

"The funny looking people—they're dressed up to play!" replied Mackie.

Heather looked in her rearview mirror, still seeing nothing. "Natalie, did you see people?"

Natalie sat up and looked out the window one more time. She said, "Back there!" pointing through the trees. "They're dancing!"

By this time, Heather was curious, but not enough to turn the car around. It was getting dark, and who knows what people do out in the sticks, she thought. They could be engaged in some weird ritual for all she knew. She drove up the hill, wondering what the kids had seen.

Suddenly, she spotted something to her left moving toward the road. She slammed on the brakes. Slowly, the figure of a woman dressed in Native American attire wafted across the road in front of her. She was vaguely transparent but solid enough that Heather could see the beads on her gown and the feathers falling down the back of her long dark hair from her headband. She seemed completely oblivious to the headlights that shined toward her, eerily piercing her body and passing through to the other side.

Heather woke her husband. "Dave, Dave! Look!" she whispered as the woman hesitated by the side of the road before vanishing into the trees.

Her husband woke just in time to catch a glimpse of the woman, and in his just waking state, he opened the car door and jumped out. "Hey, are you alright?" he called.

The woman did not turn or acknowledge his presence but continued her disappearance among the trees.

The stories of people along the road and crossing the road in this area are plentiful. We hear from people on the tour now and then that they've had this experience, and they ask us if we know anything about the haunting of the area. We don't know who the spirits are, but we think they could be the ghost dancers of the 1890s.

The area in and around Fort Collins has only been populated by those of non-native descent for a short time in history. The fur traders, most of French descent, began frequenting the area in the 1830s. Antoine Janis, the first non-native white settler, traveled through the area in 1836 with his father. He found the area so beautiful that he returned and began the town of Colona (later LaPorte) in 1858. Like many of his fellow fur traders, he married a young Sioux maiden of the Oglala Sioux tribe. Intermarriage between the fur traders and the tribes became a fairly common and accepted practice during that time, and one would think that this would have encouraged the American government to be more sympathetic to the plight of the tribes. It did not.

Prior to the 1800s, the Arapahoe and Cheyenne used this area as a hunting ground. Buffalo and deer were plentiful. In most years, their people ate well and had plenty.

In the early to mid-1800s, white settlers and travelers who were headed toward the California gold rush began to frequent this area. They probably meant no harm, and most of them were just passing through. Unfortunately, they brought with them diseases that were unfamiliar to the native population and for which the tribes carried no immunity whatsoever. In the 1840s, measles, whooping cough and cholera took their toll on the Native American population. Some estimates say that half the local Cherokee Nation died during these epidemics.

But disease was not the only harm the influx of settlers inflicted on the native population. They brought domesticated cattle to graze on the plains, pushing the native buffalo from traditional hunting grounds. Homesteading took these sacred hunting grounds and deeded them to immigrants, who turned the area into agricultural fields. The Native American population was continually being displaced, disrespected and starved of their precious resources.

Tensions between the tribes and the settlers began to escalate. The American government established Camp Collins to oversee the safety of white settlers who flocked to the area and began an agricultural colony. The more settlers arrived, the more the resources and rights of the tribes eroded.

Native American tribes began to rebel, and battles between the American government and the people who had wandered this land for thousands of years ensued. In the Battle of Sand Creek, a wholesale slaughter of the Native American population included the torture and killing of women and children, as well as their men. Other battles took their toll, and it was clear that the ways and traditional life the Native Americans had enjoyed were now gone.

In 1878, the American government decreed that all Native Americans in the Fort Collins area (and other areas as well) relocate to designated reservations. Many of the local tribal members were moved to the Pine Ridge Reservation in the north. Many men had married Native American women, and they were told they could either abandon their wives or go live with them on the reservation. It was an excruciating choice, but many men left their homesteads, jobs and most of their assets and followed their wives to the reservation. Antoine Janis went with his wife to Pine Ridge, leaving the place he had declared "the loveliest place on earth." He died in 1890 just before the Battle of Little Bighorn.

Seeing very little light in their future, the Native Americans turned to spiritual beliefs to combat the hopelessness of their situation. A man from Nevada who called himself a prophet said that if the tribes engaged in ghost dancing, they would win back all they had lost. Ghost dancing would appeal to the spirits, who would make the whites disappear, resurrect the dead ancestors of the tribes and restore the valued and traditional way of life of the Native Americans.

The ghost dance mimicked the earlier circle dances of the tribes, and the participants dressed in full traditional regalia with paint, beads and feathers. Drums heralded the beat of the dance, and hope once again entered the lives of the tribal members.

Alas, the ghost dance did not save or restore the earthly existence of the Native American tribes. We believe that the spirits of the ancestors still dance, though, in the area north of Fort Collins. We hope that in death they have become free and that their lands and proud way of life are restored to them.

An Encounter with a Ghost Horse and Rider

There was no more necessary relationship in the 1800s than that between a man and his horse. Horses were more than just transportation. They were trusted friends to talk to on the long lonely trail, hunting partners for the roaming braves riding bareback and fellow warriors when battle between tribes broke out.

Back then, wild mustangs roamed the ranges in northern Colorado and southern Wyoming. These mighty steeds had been brought over by Spaniards in days long gone, and their progeny ran free across the plains. Strong, beautiful and proud, these horses were prized partners of the local tribes when they could be tamed.

The wise and savvy tribes would set traps to lure the horses into makeshift corrals and then release the older ones, keeping those young enough to tame and ride. In those days, the life span of a man wasn't so terribly much longer than that of a horse, and many tribesmen considered their horses lifelong friends. When they went on to the spirit world, they believed their horses would be there, too, so in their hearts and minds the friendship was for eternity.

It is no surprise, then, to occasionally encounter a ghostly spirit astride a horse, happily sharing the afterlife with his trusted mount. North of Fort Collins, near the trails that many a settler and Native American traveled throughout the past 150 years, a woman and her daughter were driving along North Highway 287. As they rounded a corner, the woman saw the ethereal image of a man on a horse crossing the road. The woman stopped the car.

"Do you see that?" she asked her daughter, doubting her own vision.

"Yes, I do!" replied her daughter.

They continued to watch as the rider and horse crossed the road in front of the car and melted into the vegetation alongside the road. She gave the following description of the event:

> *The one thing that was extremely odd when we came across this horse and rider up on 287 (other than the fact that we were out in the middle of nowhere) was that this cowboy was dressed extremely odd for today. His chaps were sort of furry, which I had never seen before, he was wearing sort of a "bowler" type hat and he was saddled on the most beautiful white horse I've ever seen. His demeanor was odd too—he just stared straight ahead as he was riding across the road, as if he didn't even see the traffic coming straight at him. Of course, if you think about it—was there even a road out there in the old days?*

The area where this happened is along the same stretch of road as the previous story, where ghost dancers were seen. We wonder if this is perhaps one of the sacred sites of the tribes who wandered the area for hundreds of years.

THE GHOST WHO TOOK A DIP IN THE SWIMMING POOL

Colorado State University's Ammons Hall

Ammons Hall on the Colorado State University campus was constructed in 1921. Known for beautiful architecture and a rich history, this building is on the National Register of Historic Places. Women's athletic programs were held there for many years, and at one time the building housed a swimming pool.

Locals tell us that many, many years ago, a young girl drowned in the pool. Ammons Hall has since been the site of many paranormal phenomena. One person mentioned the apparition of a young woman who walks up the stairs and disappears near the top. Another told us the following story of a security guard who thought she was tracking an intruder but found only a ghost.

The security guard was on duty alone one cold, snowy night many years ago when the alarm went off in the indoor pool area. She radioed in to dispatch that she would check on it and headed on over to Ammons Hall. She suspected that a group of students had weaseled their way into the building to use the indoor pool, and she was determined to find out who they were. This wasn't the first time the alarm had been tripped, but previous investigations into the building had yielded nothing. The alarm had been checked and was functioning properly. No persons were ever found intruding in Ammons Hall after the alarm had summoned security. Tonight, she thought, I am nearby, and they won't have time to run. Plus, she had the advantage of new snow. Anyone who ran would leave footprints, and she could track them down.

As she approached the entrance, she held the dispatch radio to her mouth and whispered, "Entering the pool building" to let the dispatcher know her position. She should have waited for backup. She knew this, but since it was very likely just students, she wasn't concerned.

She edged into the entry hall and heard splashing in the pool area next door. She hurried across the large entry, thinking she had caught the intruders red-handed. By the time she reached the pool area, there was no one in the pool, but there was a single set of small, wet footprints leading into the other room.

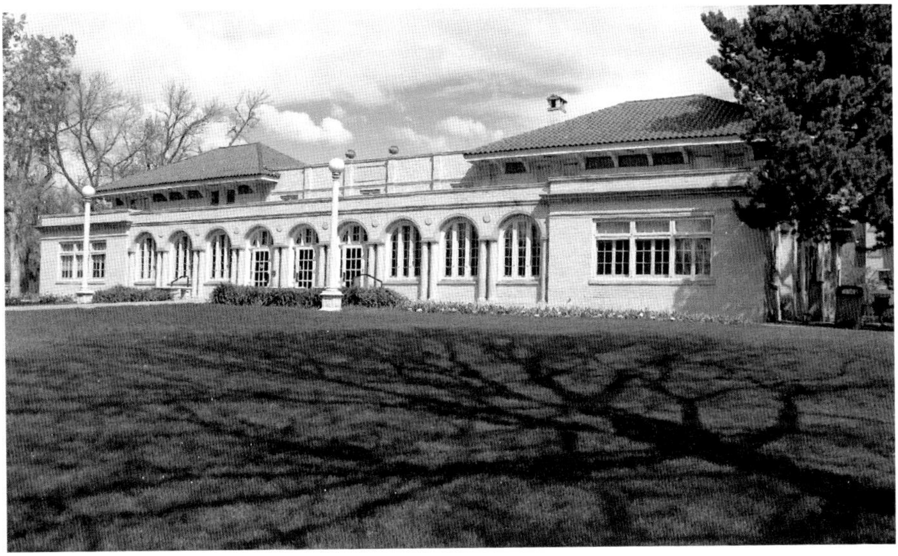

Ammons Hall.

Trailing the footprints, the security guard entered the adjacent room just in time to see the closet door close. The footprints led right into the closet, and she thought, "Aha! Gotcha!"

She again spoke into the radio to describe the situation and to let the dispatcher know she was approaching the closet and was planning to open it. Once at the closet door, she implored the student to come out, but hearing no response, she grabbed the doorknob and opened the door herself. She was shocked to find the closet empty. She turned around to check but found no wet footprints exiting the closet.

She checked the outside doors. All were locked with deadbolts from the inside. If someone had exited the closet, he or she was still in Ammons Hall. But why were there no wet footprints leading out of the closet? There was certainly no time to dry off, change and then escape in the few seconds it took the security guard to cross the room.

When another security guard arrived, they inspected every corner, nook, cranny and closet of Ammons Hall. They canvassed the exterior of Ammons Hall, and no footprints were found on the fresh snow. The young girl was never found, and to this day, there is no explanation. Were the wet footprints from a person who hid so well she couldn't be found or were they from some otherworldly apparition just enjoying a dip in the pool? We will probably never know the answer.

OLD FORT COLLINS HIGH SCHOOL AND ODD PARANORMAL SIGHTS

1400 Remington
(now the University Center for the Arts on the CSU campus)

Dark shadows fall across the rooms of this old school, and voices of students long since passed echo through the halls. Fraught with legends and stories, this place has been a "dare you to go there" destination for a few generations of teen ghost hunters.

The building itself is quite beautiful and has been restored by Colorado State University to its original splendor. If you stand in front of this building and look up, you'll see a tower where it is rumored a young student leapt to her death.

We recently spoke to someone who works in the building, and she tells us that she has never been able to find access to the tower. Other reports from locals tell us that there is a secret series of ladders that lead to the tower, but you have to be able to squeeze through a maze of crawlspaces and vent-sized openings to get there. Once there, it seems the size of the access points become smaller as one tries to navigate his or her way back down, and one long-ago student (now a grandmother) said that in her younger days, she thought she might get stuck as she tried to make her way back to the ground level.

Locals who were curious about the old school before it was restored have reported sneaking in during the dead of night to explore the halls, lofts, auditorium and basement rooms. The basement resembled a dungeon, and reports say that the windows of the basement had handprints the size of a young child, although at that point the building was vacant. Each time they visited, the handprints appeared fresh and were in different places and positions. They felt they were being watched when they were in the basement, and the sound of a small child's chuckle sent shivers up and down their spines.

Up in the music room and auditorium, there are those who heard the screaming of a young man. When they investigated, they never found anyone there. However, they would see eerie shadows moving across the walls of the auditorium, as if someone were passing in front of the moonlit windows and casting a shadow against the other side of the room. There was

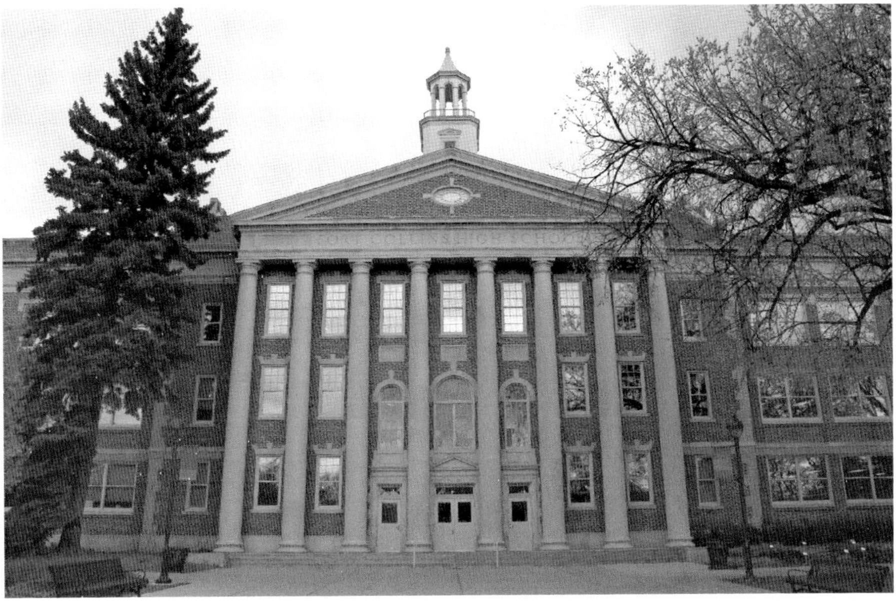

Old Fort Collins High School.

never anyone visible between the windows and the walls, which led many to believe it was the young man's ghost.

Now the building houses artists and musicians and a rebirth of culture within its walls. Whether the spirits still haunt the building is up for debate, but we can only imagine they would stay on and enjoy the beauty and culture that now surrounds them.

Beloved Ghosts of the Railroad Station

The lack of adequate transportation to Fort Collins restricted growth in the early days. Covered wagons made their way across the plains, but the roads leading to this area were rougher than many. Deep ruts and frequent mud often made these roads impassable or at the very least difficult. This may explain why the founders of the choice city were known for their perseverance and grit; the more timid and weak would have taken an easier route and likely landed in another locale.

The first railroad reached Fort Collins in 1877, and it opened the door to substantial growth. Mills and agricultural pursuits grew around the railroad, and communication with the outside world came in and out of the community with every train that passed through.

The railroad station built in 1906 still stands over on Jefferson Street and is now the home of Rodizio Grill. For decades, every soldier who left to find his destiny or returned home from war did so from the loading deck of that building. It's no surprise that some of that energy still lurks out on the loading deck.

Employees of Rodizio Grill tell us that from time to time they've heard footsteps out on the deck when taking a break. One employee swears she saw a man in an old-time military uniform pacing up and down the deck, as if impatiently waiting for the train.

From 1934 to 1948, folks leaving on the train or arriving on the train were greeted by Annie, a polite and very social mixed-breed dog that was adopted by the railroad staff and adored by the community. There is a monument to Annie outside the main Poudre Library branch near Old Town, and Annie's grave is still lovingly kept up within a small picket fence outside the Fort Collins Transit Center.

We've heard stories of Annie's ghost still happily running up to the train as the doors open, tail wagging, waiting for newcomers to exit.

There have been debates through history about whether our pets go into the hereafter with us or their lives just end. Annie and other beloved pets whose spirits have been seen or experienced after passing give us hope and belief that we will once again be reunited with our four-legged friends.

The train still runs through Fort Collins several times a day and remains a staple of the community.

LEGENDS OF THE AREA

THE HELL TREE

There are many legends associated with Fort Collins that have no historical basis. The legend of the Hell Tree is one of them.

According to local folklore, the Hell Tree is located either near LaPorte or on the other side of town near Strauss Cabin Road, where the remains of George Strauss's cabin rest. Legend states that the tree stands in the front yard of a home that was owned for years by a goat farmer. We have found no connection between Strauss's cabin and any goat farmer in the history of the area, but here is the legend:

The goat farmer was known to be a mentally unstable, temperamental man who was feared by his farmhands, his neighbors and his own family.

One day, he caught one of his farmhands stealing from him and dragged him to what is now known as the "Hell Tree" in his front yard. He threw a noose around the man's neck and, before the man could react, hoisted him up toward a limb where he was hanged to death.

Over the years, the goat farmer hanged a number of his farmhands from the Hell Tree for various "crimes" they either committed or were imagined to have committed. The people of the town became suspicious when one by one his farmhands went missing, and an inquiry was planned.

The goat farmer realized his reign of terror was coming to an end and that he likely would be imprisoned. He would not stand for this. Late one evening, he waited for his wife to draw her bath. As soon as she had settled into the warm water, he walked into the bathroom with his shotgun and killed her. He proceeded to kill the rest of his family and then went out to the front yard.

As he stood before the Hell Tree, he contemplated all the evil he'd done in his lifetime, and he slowly climbed up the limbs of the tree until he reached the highest, strongest limb where the noose had been tied. He quietly placed the noose around his neck and jumped off of the limb, ending his life.

Local teens and college students tell this story and go searching for the legendary Hell Tree. The large cottonwood tree outside the old Strauss cabin is a favorite site for telling the legend, and stories abound about spirits and apparitions being seen around the tree and in the windows of the abandoned cabin.

The following is the real history of the Strauss cabin:

George Strauss was one of the original non-native settlers of the Cache la Poudre Valley. He came to the area in May 1860, relocating from Kentucky and Indiana Territories, where he was raised. Strauss settled southeast of present-day Fort Collins and began a vegetable farm.

At that time, the population of the area was centered in the town of LaPorte, a few miles northwest along the Overland Trail. In order to sell his vegetables to folks in LaPorte without having to make the trip, he would set baskets of vegetables alongside the trail on the edge of his property. A courier would pick up the veggies on the way to LaPorte each week and drop off the cash under a rock on the way back.

The epic flood of 1864 caused extensive damage to Strauss's farm and should have served as a warning to the Strauss family about risking life and limb living in the Poudre River flood plain. However, they continued to live and farm there.

Four decades later, the Poudre once again overflowed, and a massive flood struck the Strauss farm. Strauss, now well into his seventies, tried to escape the flood but became trapped against a fence and was stranded all night. A neighbor found him in the morning, but George Strauss died later that day from the hypothermia and exposure he had suffered all night in the floodwaters.

Teens out for a night of adventure have reported seeing apparitions in the yard and in the windows of the Strauss cabin. Could it be George, who lived there all his adult life, just tending to his farm?

What Lies Beneath Old Town: The Legendary Tunnels

Fort Collins is fraught with rumors of underground tunnels throughout the Old Town area. Some say they were used for bootlegging (and no doubt that is at least somewhat correct). Some have told us they were used to house and route cattle, which seemed absurd at first but, given the cold winters and the lack of shelter in the 1800s, became a little more plausible. Some say the tunnels were used by prostitutes to travel from their houses of ill repute to the local hotels so reputable businessmen could receive these ladies of the night without being seen in the red-light district.

There is also contention by some that the tunnels do not exist and that they are just romantic rumors concocted by those with wild imaginations.

The truth may lie somewhere in between. We have heard that Colorado State University has a policy that any students caught in the tunnels will be immediately expelled. This is for safety reasons. There are verified tunnels underneath CSU that are used for access to utilities. Steam heat is transported through pipes in these tunnels from the local steam plant. If one of those pipes were to burst, any human below ground could meet a quick and painful death.

It could be that the tunnels underneath Old Town serve the same purpose and hold the same safety risks. We also know that at least one of the underground tunnels, leading to a large bunker of a room, was reinforced during the 1950s as a nuclear fallout shelter.

Many of the tunnels whose existence has been verified are no longer accessible. Entrances to these tunnels have been bricked over to ensure that no one wanders into them. One such tunnel linked the old underground jail beneath Happy Lucky's Teahouse and the area where the Silver Grill Café now sits.

Legend has it that this tunnel was used to transport jail prisoners from the cells to the mess hall, where they would take their meals chained by their ankles to the foot railings below the stools. There were other tunnels that supposedly branched off the tunnel used to transport the prisoners, and these are rumored to have led to Pine Street and even across Walnut to the area underneath the Northern Hotel.

According to local folklore, one day the jailers transported six prisoners from the jail through the tunnel to the mess hall and then after the meal walked them back through the tunnel to their cell. Upon arriving back at the jail, the guards found that they were short one prisoner. There were only five instead of six! Did the sixth prisoner quietly duck into one of the other tunnels along the way? The guards launched a search, but the man was never found. He either escaped through the tunnels or became lost in the dark and convoluted tunnel system and died in there eventually.

Several photos taken underneath Old Town in basements that were connected by those tunnels have shown apparitions of a man. Could this be the missing prisoner? He is almost always found behind a fence that separates parts of the basement morgue. We have never been able to figure out why there is a fence there, but we do wonder if this is the man's most likely view of the world after spending years behind bars.

Many of the basements throughout the Old Town region have door-sized areas that are bricked over, as if they led somewhere else at one time. Employees of the businesses loathe trips to the basement for supplies and report that they feel they're being watched. Many times, voices and footsteps are heard in these basements, but no earthly form is visible from where the voices and the footsteps emanate. Often, cold spots hover near the bricked-over areas.

One employee reported hearing a rapping sound from the other side of the brick wall covering one of the entrances. When the employee yelled, "Who's there?" a growling voice replied, "Get out of here!" Another employee told us that boxes and supplies near the same area are consistently moved around, rearranged and sometimes just tossed about the rest of the room between the time the employees and store owners go home at night and when they come back in the morning.

A locally famous hoax was played on the community decades ago when a mischievous journalist, Bob Terrill of the *Poudre Magazine* (November 1982), wrote an article on the "Underground Subway of Fort Collins." He even included a picture of one of the outside stairways leading down to the "subway station." The report said that an eleven-mile underground subway system operated from 1904 to 1918. He described his tour of the tomblike caverns left by the subway in his 1982 article, adding that the city might consider turning this area into a concept mall or a fallout shelter.

Many people, even longtime locals, believed the story, and the city of Fort Collins was plagued by questions about the "historic" subway for years.

We may believe in ghosts, but we're not buying the subway story!

A Speakeasy Frozen in Time

There is an entire block of Old Town that sits atop a maze of basements, pass-throughs, tunnels that have been bricked over to prevent access and supposedly bricked-up rooms that haven't been seen by humans for decades.

Employees of the establishments above this underground maze consistently tell us that they feel like they're being watched when they go down into the basements to retrieve supplies or to store equipment. Workers in one store laughingly told us that they use "rock, paper, scissors" to determine which unlucky soul will have to take something down to their basement.

One store owner told us that a few decades ago, one of the bricked-over entrances was knocked down so a utility crew could access the area. When the dust settled, they walked into a perfectly preserved speakeasy. Glasses still sat on the tables and the bar. Chairs were pushed back from tables, some knocked over. Dishes were in the sink, and a hand towel was carelessly tossed over the railing above the bar. It looked as if the police might have staged a raid, chased everyone out of the illegal operation and immediately had it bricked up so business wouldn't start right back up again.

The store owner continued to say that the organization that opened this area (no one knows if it was the City of Fort Collins or a utility company) just cleaned it out and once again bricked over the entrance. It makes sense to deny access—many of the older underground areas are decrepit and unsafe. But we question why no one took pictures of this "preserved moment in history" and why no one wrote about it.

Like so many stories we heard, we found nothing in the archives about this, and upon calling the City of Fort Collins, we found no one who had heard of it. Still, when wandering the basements and pass-throughs of that block, it does appear that there is at least one bricked-over entrance that could lead to a larger room.

The hauntings of the block above are so prevalent, and the stories of the store owners and employees so consistent up and down the block, that we can't deny something is going on. Books fall off shelves in the local bookstore during the night—often the same books, as if the ghosts have favorites. One store that sells ladies' accessories often has purses on the floor when employees come in some mornings.

An area we've visited underneath the Astoria used to go right out underneath the sidewalk and a bit under College Avenue. An apparition of a man in a gray pinstriped suit has been seen ducking around the corner into this dirt alcove and now has recently been seen in the basement of the Astoria. The alcove was recently covered over with concrete, so yet another isolated space lurks beneath the block.

Is the speakeasy a legend or another piece of history that has been lost through time?

THE ARAPAHOE LEGEND OF HORSETOOTH ROCK

If you look to the west above Horsetooth Reservoir, you'll see the large and interesting outcropping of rock known as Horsetooth Rock. It's visible from many areas of Fort Collins, although it looks gray from a distance, and much of the rock formation is actually fairly red.

How did a rock become sculpted to look like a horse's tooth? The Arapahoe legend tells us that there was once a giant who presided over the area, calling it the "Valley of Contentment." The giant protected the animals living there from all harm, and they could not be hunted. If anyone were to enter the valley with the intent of harming the animals, death would "rain down upon them."

In time, a great drought came upon the land outside the valley, and all the animals that the local tribes once hunted moved on in search of water. The people of the tribes were without meat and began to starve. They decided to brave the giant in order to hunt the plentiful buffalo, deer and antelope roaming the Valley of Contentment.

The tribes gathered and planned their hunt. They would wait until the Hunter's Moon, as they knew the giant was weakest when the moon was bright. Before embarking on their hunting journey, they chanted and called on the magic of their ancestors to provide them with the tools they needed. A tomahawk was sent from the heavens, and the tribes bestowed on it enchantments until the time they had waited for was at hand.

Chief Maunamoku led his warriors to the valley in search of the giant and found him sleeping atop the mountain. The chief took the magic tomahawk and heaved it over the chest of the sleeping giant, sinking it deep into his heart. He again raised the tomahawk and sliced back into the giant's chest, killing the giant and turning him into stone. His blood ran freely down into the valley.

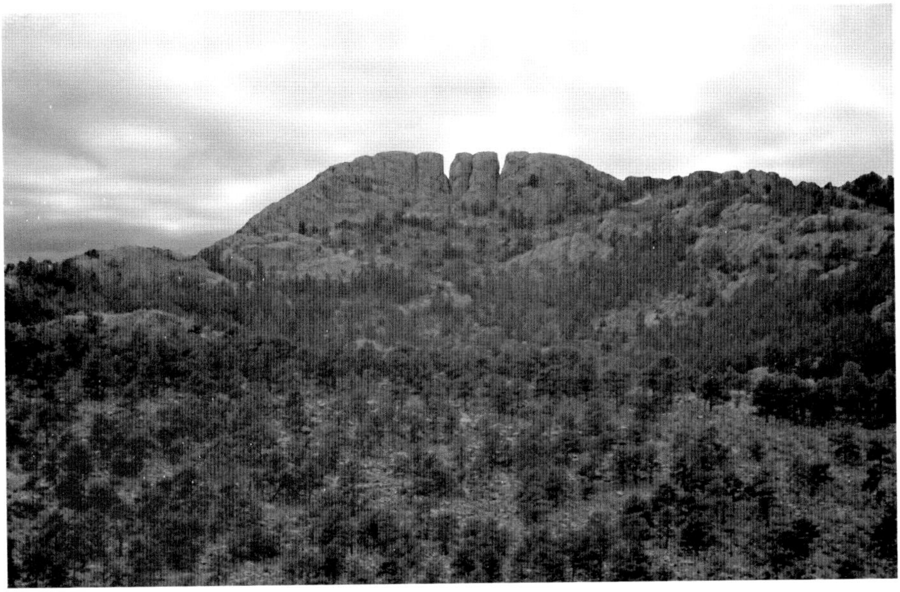

Horsetooth Rock.

The giant is now Horsetooth Rock, and the slices of his chest reflect the formation of the rock. The red color comes from the giant's blood.

There are no more buffalo in the valley and many fewer deer and antelope. The Valley of Contentment is no more, and the tribes have been banished to reservations and replaced with a new people who frequently disrespect the land.

When the thunderheads come over the mountains and descend on Horsetooth Rock, many think it could be the spirit of the slain giant rumbling his anger and striking the valley below with rods of lightning in retribution for the slaughter of his animals and the theft of his valley.

Waiting Until the Cows Come Home

One of the strangest phenomena we've heard of while gathering stories has to do with driving cattle.

Fort Collins was built on agriculture and ranching. Drovers used to drive the cattle right up Jefferson Street, leaving clouds of dust and thousands of hoofprints in their wake. The sound of the cattle running down the street was deafening, and locals likened it to thunder.

We're told that every few years, the sound of hooves barreling down Jefferson Street will be heard by those on the side of the road. Cars have been known to pull over as drivers wonder what the loud sound might be. We questioned whether the train, which runs parallel to Jefferson Street, might be the culprit. We were assured that this possibility had been ruled out and that anyone who actually heard the commotion would swear it echoed the sound of large herds of cattle running down the street.

There have been similar reports up and down College Avenue.

Another odd legend says that the tunnels and large rooms underneath the city were dug to house cattle during the brutal winters. Some of the tunnels were only a few feet tall and meant to route cattle from a big underground room in the 200 block of South College Avenue to the stockyards and the train station a few blocks away. We've even been told we can find this in the local historical archives, but so far we have found nothing about this.

The large room underneath South College is now a series of basements, and locals who have worked for the businesses above these basements report seeing apparitions of men in old-time business suits and hearing voices coming from basement rooms that are empty. Like workers from the next block north, they report a sense of being watched as the go about their business in these basement rooms, and most attend to their business downstairs and hurry back to ground level as fast as they can.

Whether the legend of cattle inhabiting this underground area is true is up for debate. We have noticed that some of the underground areas are built with really low ceilings, which would back up this claim, but we also realize this may be because the areas weren't built to house people but rather for storage.

In any case, cattle were a huge part of the early Fort Collins life and economy. They had their place above ground, possibly below ground and certainly in the history and lore of the community.

CONCLUSION

Fort Collins Tours hopes you have enjoyed this collection of stories. Clearly, there is more going on in Fort Collins than meets the eye.

We hope you will come along with us on one of our journeys underneath Old Town and experience these places for yourself. Who knows, you might even encounter a ghost or two. Tickets can be purchased online at www.hauntedfortcollins.com.

If you have ghost stories, legends or have had experiences yourself, we would love to hear about them. You can reach us at www.hauntedfortcollins.com, and you can also check out communications and photos on our Facebook page, also called Haunted Fort Collins.

We would like to thank the many people who contributed to this book with their generous time and storytelling. To our crew of guides—Melissa, Brie, Shane, Brian, Josh, Jake and Sammy—we couldn't have done any of this without you! Thank you for all your work telling the stories and often gathering stories for the tours and for this book. Special thanks to Samantha Holland for editing parts of the book and to Shane Sheridan for bringing us stories we wouldn't have otherwise encountered.

To the businesses that were kind enough to let us mention them in the book and continually let us bring groups of people through their doors and into their basements, thank you so much for your partnership. Your generous sharing of your space, time and stories is much appreciated.

To the young men of Sigma Phi Epsilon, we extend our thanks for your hospitality and your stories.

We also want to thank Janet Smith, daughter of the pilot in the Armadillo Garage story, for her years of research and her willingness to let us include some of it in the book; Kim Pentecost, the intuitive in a couple of the stories, for her kindness and sharing of her experiences; Rose Glenn for sharing her story of the ghost rider and horse; and all others who shared stories along the way.

Lastly, thank you to The History Press for asking us to write this book and for supporting and educating us along the way.

—Chris, Laurie, Robin, Jake and Lori Juszak of Fort Collins Tours, Inc.

About the Author

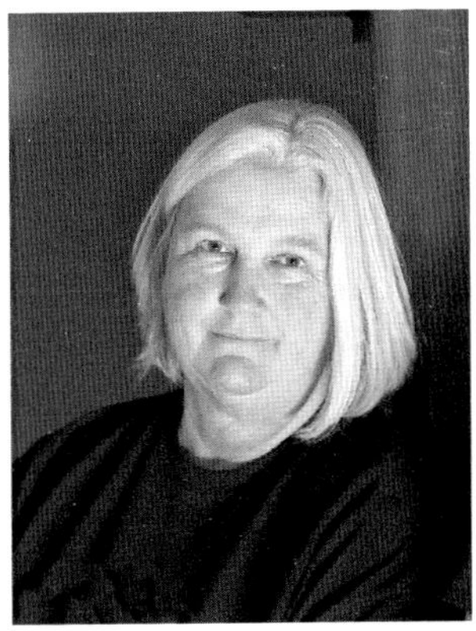

The Juszak family owns Fort Collins Tours, Inc. Together, they researched, developed and implemented the Haunted Fort Collins Ghost Tours and Historic Fort Collins Tours.

Lori Juszak, MBA, teaches at Front Range Community College and is an avid museum and history buff. She spends a good deal of time around and underneath Old Town Fort Collins leading tours and exploring the history and hauntings of the area. She also teaches classes in paranormal studies and parapsychology.

Chris Juszak, who provided the majority of the photos for this book, holds a bachelor's of science in computer science.

Visit us at
www.historypress.net

This title is also available as an e-book